You're Going To Do What?!

Helping You Understand the Homeschool Decision

BY LAURAJEAN DOWNS

You're Going To Do What?
Helping You Understand the Homeschool Decision

ISBN 1-888306-17-3
Copyright © 1997 by Laurajean Downs
Published by Holly Hall Publications, Inc.
229 South Bridge Street
P. O. Box 254
Elkton, MD 21922-0254
Tel. (888) 669-4693

Send requests for information to the above address.

Cover & book design by Mark Dinsmore
Arkworks@aol.com

All Scripture quotations are taken from the Holy Bible,
New International Version and King James Version.

Printed in the United States of America

TO VERN,
MY LIFELONG PARTNER
AND CONSTANT FRIEND.

Table of Contents

Preface

How does a family's decision to homeschool affect the extended family? The responses of various relatives vary widely, but often the decision to homeschool results in a family crisis.

Grandparents are confused or up in arms, well-meaning aunts or cousins are worried, and the mother and father, who are trying to do their best for their children, feel defensive, uncertain, and resentful that their family has so little faith in them that they doubt their ability to teach their own children. Wanting to avoid arguments and confrontations, children and parents alike call each other less frequently and the time between visits seems to get longer and longer. Everyone suffers, but the grandchildren suffer most of all, because they are denied one of life's most special joys—that of knowing and enjoying their grandparents.

My husband and I have four children, three of whom are currently being homeschooled. Becoming a homeschool family was a slow process for us, and I tiptoed around it for quite some time, finally embarking upon it with more doubts and questions than convictions and answers. Not the least of my worries was what I would tell my family, and what would happen if they didn't support us. Because I didn't want to approach them with an emotional speech, I wrote up a list of the reasons we had decided to try it and what we hoped to accomplish. I thought that if I could present my case to our family in a logical manner, they would at least be receptive to what we were doing.

The day of my "presentation" I sat everyone down and stumbled through my sheet. Instead of coming across as a confident teacher who could easily accomplish her task, I felt like a criminal trying to defend my record. At that point, I determined to find a more effective way to communicate my choice to my family. My little speech to my family was the seed from which this book grew.

In writing this book, I read widely from the available literature on homeschooling. I read about the legal aspects, the philosophical foundation, and the history of homeschooling and public schooling. I read studies designed to evaluate the effectiveness of homeschooling, and the advantages of family rather than peer socialization. I interviewed homeschoolers and their parents, two of whom—Dorothy Ferguson and Polly Gilpin—will be sharing with you through these pages both their initial responses to the news that their children had decided to homeschool, and their eventual approbation and support of their children's endeavor.

This book is a guide to help the families of home-schoolers understand the homeschool movement in general and to offer some insight into the reasons certain of their family members—convinced that homeschooling is the right answer for them—have opted for this seemingly unorthodox form of schooling. Possession of the facts can do much to relieve fears and anxieties.

Ultimately, I hope the book will enable parents to support their children in their homeschooling endeavor. More than that, I hope it will encourage them to become active participants in the great work of educating their grandchildren. Homeschooling is such an intrinsic part of family life that grandparents (and aunts, uncles, and cousins) have an unparalleled opportunity to play a huge role in this process.

I wish to thank all who played a role in the writing of this book. I thank my Lord and Saviour Jesus Christ, who has the grace to save even me. I thank my husband for always believing in me, for providing me with four beautiful children to homeschool, and for his constant support of my writing. I thank my parents for raising me with wisdom and love and giving me the confidence to tackle projects that look daunting at first. A special note of thanks also goes to my "other parents," who have been faithful and encouraging, and who are model grandparents. Although my children have not completely understood what it meant when I told them Mommy was "writing a book," I want to thank them for their love and support anyway, and for giving me endless amounts of material and inspiration.

Also, I want to thank my many friends in Cheyenne, Wyoming, who watched my children and encouraged me, even though I was preparing to move to another state! And thank you to Nancy Drazga, who has looked at this manuscript more than I ever wanted to, and has made it a much better book. Finally, thanks also go to all the people I have encountered over the years, who have given me stories and shared with me their experiences of homeschooling their children: you have been an inspiration to my husband and myself in the raising of our children for the Lord.

Introduction

CHILDREN'S CHILDREN ARE A CROWN
TO THE AGED, AND PARENTS ARE THE PRIDE
OF THEIR CHILDREN. —PROVERBS 17:6

Your family is gathering for their annual Fourth of July get-together at Green Acres Park. As you and your husband drive up to the picnic ground, various games are already underway: volleyball over by the swings, a very rambunctious game of tag, and even a game of horseshoes on the other side of the picnic tables. The day is hot, but a nice breeze is keeping everyone relatively cool.

Your husband parks the car and helps you carry the cooler over to the picnic tables, where you open the lid of the cooler and take out the potato salad and deviled eggs—your specialties—making sure that the root beer is still cold. Root beer is the drink of choice for one of your young granddaughters, and warm root beer just will not do.

Placing your dishes on the table, already filled with fried chicken, salads of all kinds, chips, vegetables, and dips, you return to the car for a blanket, lay it out in a nice shady spot, and join the food line that is already forming around the row of picnic tables. Filling your plate, you settle yourself on your blanket, pleased that everyone seems to be enjoying themselves.

Leaning over to your husband, you say wistfully, "Am

I just getting old, or do these reunions get better every year?"

Smiling, he answers, "You're not getting old, and they do get better. I love watching all the children play."

"I do, too. Look at Janice and Michael playing leap frog over there. Aren't they dear?"

When you've decided you can't eat another bite, you say to your husband, "I think I'll go over and talk to Karen about her plans for school next year."

Helping you to your feet, he responds with a grin, "Good idea. I think I'll go see how my horseshoe arm is holding up."

You wander over to the swings, where Karen, your daughter-in-law, is enjoying the sun and watching the children play. Putting your arm around her shoulders, you give her a little squeeze. "I'm glad you could make it today," you tell her.

"Oh, I wouldn't miss the Fourth of July picnic for the world," she says.

"I was watching Janice and Michael playing leap frog," you tell her. "They look so sweet playing together. Aren't you glad you've been able to stay home with them during their early years?"

"Yes, Mom, I've been very thankful for that. It's impressed upon me more and more each day what a responsibility Eric and I have to raise these kids right. The world is pretty messed up these days."

"Janice must be very excited to be starting kindergarten this fall. Have you taken her to the school to look around yet?"

Karen pauses. "Well, Mom, Eric and I were going to talk to you and Dad about this tonight, after the picnic. But since you asked about school, I may as well tell you now. We're planning to homeschool Janice this year."

You feel yourself drawing away, and then turning so you can face your daughter-in-law squarely. "You're going to do *what?*"

"Teach her at home," repeats Karen. "Lots of people are doing it these days. The public schools just aren't what they were when you were a child, and we believe God would have us train and teach her at home."

Karen's voice and the noise of the children playing grow dim, as you struggle to comprehend what you have just heard. It doesn't make sense! Things were going so well. Eric was doing so well at his new job, they were fixing up the house they'd just bought, and now THIS!!!!

* * * * *

Are you the grandmother in this scene?

Are you bewildered, confused, and distrustful, filled with as many doubts as your children seem to be armed with convictions?

In various forms, this scenario has occurred thousands of times in small towns, suburbs, and cities across the nation, because each year, ever-growing numbers of parents choose to homeschool their children. Homeschool parents come from all walks of life and from many different backgrounds, both cultural and religious. Christians as well as non-Christians have decided homeschooling is the best course for their families. Doctors, teachers, salesmen, plumbers—people from all walks of life—are choosing to homeschool. In ever-increasing numbers, women are returning home from the workplace, or simply choosing not to enter it at all until their children are grown. Some women even start businesses at home so they can help with the family's finances and still be at home to teach their children.

As the number of homeschooling families grows, so does the number of bewildered grandparents who are wondering exactly what is going on with their children. Homechooling just doesn't seem to make sense, as far as they're concerned, at least not for *their* grandchildren. Won't they turn out weird if they don't go to school? How will anyone know whether they're learning what they're supposed to be learning? What's wrong with public schools, anyway? And how will they ever manage home-schooling on top of the two toddlers, the housework, and everything else they are doing—not to mention living on one income? The list of questions could go on and on— the same list of questions, in fact, that your children addressed before they decided to homeschool.

Dorothy Ferguson and her sister, Polly Gilpin, are two grandmothers who once had these same questions and concerns. Dorothy lives on a family-owned ranch near Cheyenne, Wyoming, where she came as a young wife. She knew the benefits of small classes and a strong family life: her children attended a one-room school-house because they lived too far from town to attend public schools. Yet when Mary Lou, her youngest child, decided to homeschool, Dorothy was distraught. Thinking Mary Lou would soon change her mind, how-ever, she decided to remain silent and wait and see what happened. In the end, it was Dorothy who changed her mind, as she saw the progress her grandson was making in his studies.

Polly Gilpin's story is similar. When I interviewed her, she said, "A few years ago homeschooling was not looked upon as something 'normal' people did," but went on to say that the number of people now involved has caused many people to revise their opinions. In her own case, her experience with her niece, Mary Lou, had given her a favorable view of homeschooling, so that when her daughter decided to homeschool, she was able to be immediately supportive.

Your children's initial interest in homeschooling was fueled by their love for their children and their desire to offer them the best education possible. Their decision to homeschool was the result of the answers they found to the same questions you are now asking. As Dorothy Ferguson and Polly Gilpin can tell you, your attitude about homeschooling is very important to your children. It is out of love for you and a desire for family unity that they want your understanding and approval of their decision to homeschool. They care very much what you think, and they wish they could effectively communicate to you their reasons for choosing to homeschool. They particularly want their children to enjoy their grandparents—as they know how special the grandparent/grandchild relationship is—and they don't want to deliberately do anything to disturb that. They feel hurt, sorrowful, and frustrated when they find that their decision has created a rift in the family.

The purpose of this book is to answer those questions that grandparents and other family members have about homeschooling. Hopefully, it will enable you to understand why parents—and particularly, the parents of your grandchildren—homeschool and to discover that it is a positive and rewarding educational option. Beyond that, its purpose is to help you strengthen your relationship with your children and grandchildren, and instill in you a desire to become an active participant in your grandchildren's homeschooling experience.

Chapter One

· · · · · · · · · · · · · · · · · · · ·

Why Homeschool? A Path to Academic Excellence

APPLY YOUR MIND TO INSTRUCTION AND YOUR
EAR TO WORDS OF KNOWLEDGE. —PROVERBS 23:12

Lynette watched her third-grade son struggle daily with his spelling and reading. Her heart ached for him as he brought home papers with failing grades, but she didn't know what to do to help him. When the teacher called and asked to see her, she knew what they would discuss in the meeting.

"Lynette, Jason just keeps falling further and further behind in spelling and reading. Have you noticed?"

Lynette nods. "Yes, his father and I have been distressed about his grades, but what can we do? He just doesn't seem to grasp many of the ideas presented."

"I think he just needs more one-on-one time with a capable teacher. Here's a list of tutors I recommend. If you will pick one you are comfortable with, and set up times for Jason to meet with her, I think his grades will begin to improve after only a few weeks. I have never sent a child to a tutor and not seen tremendous improvement."

Lynette smiles and breathes a sigh of relief. "Oh, thank you! I hadn't even considered that. I'll call this afternoon." As Lynette walks to her car, she remembers the homeschool mother she talked to in the supermarket last winter, and wonders if she could tutor Jason herself.

* * * * *

Although the reasons families choose to homeschool are many, they can be grouped into three general categories: the desire for quality education, the rewards of the homeschooling lifestyle, and the direction given to them in God's word.

For most parents it is very important that their children succeed academically—a concern that grandparents also share (and one that is heightened when the family decides to begin homeschooling). Ironically, it is often a child's failure in public school—usually academic—that causes parents to take the plunge into homeschooling. As long as their children are doing tolerably well in school, many people favorably disposed towards homeschooling are reluctant to take that first step. It is often only the urgency created by an academic crisis that propels many into what they often tell themselves is only a "temporary" situation. However, as the parents grow comfortable in their new roles, and see their children thriving in the new academic environment, what was meant to be a temporary measure becomes a firmly established way of life. Beginning with the idea that they will get their children "back on track," and then put them back in school, they soon begin to experience additional benefits of teaching their children at home that they hadn't originally thought too much about. Thus, for yet another family, homeschooling becomes a permanent way of life.

Tutoring: The One-On-One Approach

Whether or not Lynette teaches Jason at home, or she and her husband hire a tutor, Jason will benefit from the tutoring, and will gain more confidence in his other subjects as well. Educational experts know that the one-on-one method of teaching children is the most effective. And the one-on-one method, or tutoring, is what homeschooling is all about.

Although we call it home "schooling," it would be more accurate to call it home "teaching." There are few similarities between children learning at home and children learning in a school situation, since the children at home are in fact tutored, and not schooled in a group. At home, the child's school day is devoted totally to instruction, because a tutor does nothing but teach. The difference between homeschooling ("tutoring" at home) and the remedial tutoring sometimes required for public school children, is that the homeschooled child is tutored in all subjects as a matter of course, rather than in one subject because he is "behind." Homeschoolers thus have all the benefits of tutoring, and none of the negative connotations, and they are tutored by their own mothers and fathers.

Let's walk through a typical lesson as it is taught in a typical homeschool. This will be a math lesson on fractions, a new subject for seven-year-old Rachel. First, Mom will lay out some colored circles that are cut into various pieces: halves, thirds, fourths, fifths, and sixths. She will let Rachel play with the shapes and put them together like puzzles for a few moments. Then she will ask her some questions.

"Rachel, how many pieces are in the blue circle?"

"Two."

"Right. There are two halves. Can you say half? If a circle is cut in half, the two pieces will always be exactly the same size. Lay one half over the other and match them up. Good. See how they are the same? If a shape has only two parts, and they are exactly the same, then it is cut in half. Now, which circle has three parts?"

The lesson continues in this manner until two or three concepts have been taught. Then Rachel will open to a page in her workbook and complete a page or two that reinforces the concepts she has just worked on. By the time she has finished, she will understand the concept, and will have practiced it, within less than half an hour.

This brief illustration exemplifies several benefits of the tutorial model that is the foundation of homeschooling: children receive one-on-one instruction, hands-on practice, immediate feedback, and instruction tailored to the way they learn.

One-On-One Versus the Classroom

Compare this with a classroom setting, where the children are to work as a group. The concepts are explained to the entire group, and some children will understand them. Then each child will practice on paper, receiving no immediate feedback. If Rachel were in a classroom, and were to finish her work early, she would be given extra work to keep her busy until the other kids had finished. If she didn't understand something, she would raise her hand and wait for the teacher to give her two or three minutes of help. If she still didn't understand, the class would probably do a similar lesson tomorrow, in the same format, and Rachel would hopefully pick it up then.

Another advantage to the tutorial method of teaching is that the pace is geared to the ability of the child. In a classroom, the pace is set for the learning ability of the average student. Those who learn faster than the average remain unchallenged, and those who learn more slowly must move on before they master the concept. When a child learns at home, he can move ahead at his own speed. In our homeschool, if we get stuck on a particular lesson, I find other ways to present the material, and we practice it more intensely. If the children are moving along well, I can move ahead to new material that is more challenging.

The tutorial method is also more beneficial in preparing children for the learning they will do as adults. Most learning at the adult level is self-paced and tailored for the adult's need for the information. An adult would consider it foolish to crawl through material he already understood. And an adult would also know when to spend extra time to master an idea if he needed to know it for his work, or he was having trouble understanding a concept. The tutorial method is not only the teaching method of choice for children, but it prepares them for the way they will educate themselves as adults.

I remember when I was growing up and attending elementary school. Every Friday I would bring home a big stack of papers that I had completed that week. My mother would look at them, and then we would put them in a box. If I had missed an answer on a test on Tuesday, I rarely learned from that mistake, because I never looked to see what I had done wrong. The only time I had consistent follow-through was when my mother sat down with me and went over my work.

But in a homeschool setting, the feedback is immediate. I check my children's work when they have finished it, before they go on to another subject. If they miss answers on a test, I go over the material with them the next day, so that I know they have learned something from their mistakes. This is one reason we like to do some of our work out loud. It takes much less time than writing, and I can still get a good idea if they have grasped the material we have studied.

Testing for Results

All of this *sounds* like good teaching, you may say, but does it work? Although remedial tutoring is well established as a viable teaching method, the results of homeschooling still need to be measured in an accurate way. Looking at a specific child's achievement can give one a good idea of how that child is doing, but in order to know if teaching methods are truly effective, there must be objective criteria to test achievement. This can be done in two ways: by examining the curriculum the child has mastered and thereby estimate a grade level, and by administering standardized tests.

Homeschoolers across the country use curricula structured with a scope and sequence of skills that follows the same patterns as public school material. Many curriculum companies go into greater detail or have more challenging material than their public school counterparts, but the core material is similar. Therefore, if a homeschool mom knows that her child has successfully completed a publisher's third grade curriculum, she knows that her child is at least on a par with a child going into fourth grade in public school.

But many homeschooling parents want to know from an objective standpoint whether their children are at grade level, so they administer standardized tests. Although standardized tests have many weaknesses in their overall evaluation of a single child, they are useful in comparing large groups of children. The tests are structured so that a child who has completed third grade will score at the 3.9 or 4.0 grade level if she is learning exactly on schedule. (The first number represents the grade year and the second number represents the month of the school year.)

Scores can also be expressed as percentiles. The national average is 50%. Therefore, if Rachel scores at the fiftieth percentile, she scored higher than fifty percent of all the students who took the test, and 49% of the students scored higher than she did. A child's test scores for individual subjects may vary, sometimes quite a bit: everyone is better at some subjects than others. But these fluctuations are used to point out areas a child needs to work on, while still providing a point of reference for what the child has learned.

How Well Do Homeschoolers Do On These Tests ?

Homeschoolers have been the subject of several studies to determine how their academic achievement compares to that of children taught in more traditional settings. The results of the studies have been consistent, and all point to the efficacy of homeschooling as a method of instruction. An article in *The Teaching Home* summarized the findings of several of these studies:

> Both the Oregon Department of Education and the Tennessee Department of Education have reported that the home educated consistently score about the average 50th percentile.
>
> Jon Wartes, a public high school counselor in Washington, has found for several years that the home educated's average score was at the 65th to 67th percentile.
>
> Dr. Brian Ray has studied the home educated in

numerous situations. He has repeatedly found the achievement test scores of the home educated in Florida, Maine, Montana, Nevada, North Dakota, Oklahoma, Utah, Virginia, Washington, nationwide in the United States and in Canada to be in the 65th to 80th percentile range, well about the national average.[1]

Another issue of *The Teaching Home* reported:

The largest-ever collection of home-educated students' test scores was recently analyzed and released. Standardized academic achievement test scores from 16,320 students in grades kindergarten through 12 for all 50 states and the District of Columbia were very high.

These achievement scores, along with research findings on social and emotional adjustment of children taught at home, continue to support the belief that home education is beneficial to children . . .

The students' average in terms of the basic battery (a combination of the three Rs) was the 77th percentile. The 77th percentile in basic battery indicates that the typical home schooler does better than 77 percent of the norming population in those subjects. (It should be noted that the national average is the 50th percentile.)[2]

It is important to remember that the very nature of standardized tests limits what they are able to measure. All questions are multiple choice and cover only the basic skills and facts taught in schools. Standardized tests cannot test creativity, writing skills, speaking skills, or anything else that cannot be measured by those multiple choice questions. Consequently, few people use them as the sole means of measuring or comparing students' achievements. Their value is that they provide an assessment of the achievement levels of a whole nation of children with regard to certain basic skills and information, and enable educators to evaluate what is being learned and what is not, at least with regard to those basic skills.

A study reported in *Marching to the Beat of Their Own Drum: A Profile of Home Education Research* measured intellectual development rather than achievement scores. David Quine and Dr. Edmund Marek compared students that had been solely home-educated with those in Pathway Schools, which are designed to promote intellectual development and sometimes include homeschoolers. Although there was no significant difference in the intellectual development of the two groups, there was the suggestion that "home educated students move into formal thought between the ages of 10 and 11, which is far earlier than the national average at ages 15 to 20."[3]

Public Schools: A Closer Look

All well and good, you say. It's nice that homeschoolers are doing well. And you can easily see the advantages of one-on-one teaching over the one-to-twenty or one-to-thirty ratios that are common in public school classrooms. But why is learning at home so much more preferable to being in a classroom with other children? What's so wrong with public school? I went to public school, and I turned out OK, you say.

Indeed, many people are taken aback when they learn that many homeschoolers have serious problems with many aspects of the public school system.

In responding, I am reminded of the way my mother took care of my brother and sister and me. When I was growing up, my mother took precautions that many people did not understand. For example, we were never allowed out in the sun for any length of time without sunscreen. I grew up in an era when lying out in the sun was a regular pastime for young girls, and the brighter the burn the happier the girl. But not in our family—sunscreen was regularly smeared over our faces and noses.

Yes, we hated it. But Mom was determined, long before there were scores of articles circulating about skin cancer and premature aging. Before anyone else took seriously the dangers of the sun's rays to unprotected skin, we were protected, and I am very glad now. When I read research that states that the number of serious burns a person had as a child will determine his odds of getting skin cancer now, I breathe a sigh of relief. Mom kept us from evils that we weren't aware of.

My mother was protective in other ways—in the matter of drinking water, for instance. When we went hiking, we were never allowed to drink from streams or rivers. We would be at very high altitudes, where the water looked crystal clear in our hands, and still she would warn us not to sip. This seemed silly.

"Look how clear that water is!" we would argue. "And it is so cold and fresh!"

But she would shake her head. "You have no idea what microorganisms could be in it. How do you know there aren't animals upstream standing in this water?"

That was usually enough to convince us. Now, many years later, I can see the wisdom of her ways. I have known people who have contracted giardiasis and other intestinal disorders from drinking bad water. I have seen the weight loss, the discomfort, and the endless trips to doctors that they endure. Although I couldn't see the danger, I am glad my mother kept us from it.

The same argument can be made with regard to the public schools. They look fine. How can anything be wrong here? The children are out playing at recess, the desks are lined up in neat little rows, and the teachers look so nice! What's the problem?

What's Actually Wrong With Public Education?

Like bad drinking water, the problems with the public school system cannot usually be seen with the naked eye. Sometimes it is not until years later that parents can look back and be glad that they protected their child from the many negative aspects of the public school system.

One has only to read the daily papers or any one of a number of national magazines to realize that the public schools are plagued by many troubles. Many of these troubles are the consequences of the problems with the concepts and principles underlying public education, as well as the inescapable nature of mass education.

Public schools today are different from the public school you may remember attending: they have gotten worse, in all kinds of ways. While I am not talking specifically about your neighborhood school down the block, which may be better or worse than the typical public school, if you look closely at your local school, you will recognize much of what is discussed here.

Although many experts disagree about the severity of the problems in the public schools, and almost everyone disagrees about the solutions, the consensus is that the public education system is in need of improvement. An article in *Business Week* summarized some of the problems with today's public education:

> Americans are fed up with public schools. Businesses complain that too many job applicants can't read, write, or do simple arithmetic. Parents fear that the schools have become violent cesspools where gangs run amok and that teachers are more concerned with their pensions than their classrooms. Economists fret that a weak school system is hurting the ability of the U.S. to compete in the global economy. And despite

modest improvements in these scores, U.S. students still rank far behind most of the international peers in science and math.

And the woes of public schools may be about to get even deeper. Over the rest of the decade, the nation's schools will face a financial crunch that will be far worse than almost anyone had projected. Tight budgets will mean overcrowded classrooms, less individual attention, deferred maintenance, and elimination of such "frills" as music, art, and sports. And schools will have difficulty paying for the computers and other information technology needed to prepare young Americans for the new workplace.[4]

The article went on to detail many of the problems now facing the public schools, and offered some ways to improve the system. One suggestion was the establishment of charter schools, which would give the public education monopoly some competition and offer parents more educational options. A review of the above paragraphs makes it obvious that homeschooling is a solution to many of the problems that exist in the public schools. Most of the drawbacks of a public classroom are simply not present in a homeschool setting. While I realize that homeschooling is not the answer for the entire nation, it could provide an answer for a large segment of the school population.

Homeschooling could help the distressed system in two ways. First, the families that homeschool would have a successful school experience, and secondly, the public school enrollment increases that are alarming the experts would taper off. The average class size in the public schools would be smaller, thus improving the classroom climate and allowing the teacher to give each student more individual attention.

Whatever the solution, this article and many others like it emphasize the fact that the public school system is an institution in need of change. In a recent article in *The Wall Street Journal,* a mother wrote about her experience with the public schools and her decision to teach her child at home:

> We gave the schools a bright, happy child, eager to learn and a joy to be near; they returned a miserable little snot who held the firm conviction that "books are stupid," and thought herself a failure. Nineteen months after my husband and I decided to teach our daughter ourselves, we again have a happy child, one who has cheerfully read her way through the "American Girl" and "Little House" books all on her own. It has not been an easy path, but is has been eminently worthwhile . . .
>
> Her school was alarming for other reasons, too. Her teachers lacked rudimentary writing skills, and sent home notes rife with spelling and grammatical errors. And current pedagogical theory demands that children be placed in small "cooperative learning" groups, with those who need help asking not the teacher but their peers. Our daughter's classmates "helped" her by telling her the answers, so she learned nothing.
>
> When my daughter did learn at school, she was taught dubious lessons. Theories about deforestation and depletion of the ozone layer were presented as fact. Recycling was elevated to a religion. She could recite a litany of praise for contemporary leaders, but she barely knew who Washington, Jefferson or Lincoln were.
>
> "Self-esteem" is the most important goal in modern education. But telling children that they're "special," without demanding that they make an effort to learn, merely teaches them that it's OK to be slackers. We wanted more than that for our daughter. We investigated private schools in the area, but found that all rely on the same pedagogical methods. We concluded that we couldn't possibly do a worse job ourselves.[5]

Does Today's Classroom Facilitate Learning?

The most obvious problem with public schools is the classroom setting, which we addressed briefly above when discussing the tutorial method used by homeschoolers. In public schools, kids must learn in a group, as a group, and progress at basically the same rate. Though this method can work for the average students, it is hard on the rest: those that learn more slowly are forced to drop a concept and move on before it is lodged in their minds, and children that learn quickly are bored by the repetition. Statistically, there will always be some who move faster or slower than the rest of the group, and so the needs of those children will always go unmet. Those in the middle—the "average" learners—will eventually pick up the information, one way or another. Also, due to the distractions and demands of a large classroom, students receive very little one-on-one time with the teacher.

When I was a public school teacher, I was frequently frustrated by the lack of individual instruction time I could spend with each child. If I had time to help a child with more than one problem a day, I was having a good day—a day on which attending to unruly children wasn't using up as much of my time as usual. On bad days, I would think of the quiet, well-behaved students, and realize I probably hadn't had any interaction with them all day long. This is very frustrating to a good teacher, but unavoidable when teaching a large group. No amount of extra money or federal changes in the system can correct problems like these: they are built into the structure of public education.

What Are They Teaching Our Kids?

In addition to the problems inherent in the structure of the classroom, there is a disturbing, philosophical change going on in classrooms. I am not saying that every teacher is bent on teaching strange philosophies to children, but rather that the entire system is shifting its focus and intent.

The focus of today's schools has shifted from the teaching of knowledge to that of helping children make choices. In other words, schools are less interested in having children learn a body of knowledge and master skills that will enable them to do so than they are in shaping attitudes. Schools are considered to be places to raise children to function in the society of the future, institutions designed to produce "politically correct" people. This means that subjects such as drug abuse education, globalism, and cultural diversity get more emphasis than what we call the "basics"—reading, writing, and arithmetic.

A parent recently went to a parent-teacher conference at the school his two children attended. New curricula were being reviewed at the meeting. The staff members, trying to explain the basic philosophies behind the proposed material, stated:

> We have discovered that it is inappropriate for our teachers to assume they know total truth. First, we have found that what is true today may not be true tomorrow. It would be presumptuous for our instructors to force today's reality down the throats of their pupils. Second, we feel that what is truth to you may not be truth to me. It is all relative. Third, we now know that we can severely damage a child's self-esteem by telling him he has the wrong answer.[6]

These statements completely overlook the fact that

children will be tested on specific information, information that does have a right and wrong answer. But this is the philosophy of moral relativism that is being promoted in the classrooms, through the textbooks, and everywhere in the media. In a nutshell, children are being taught that there are no absolute values or correct answers, that everything just changes with the times.

The Public Schools: Purveyors of Moral Relativism

Moral relativism may not be anything new, but it is being presented in some new and troubling ways. Specifically, it is being presented to public school children through textbooks, and through special classes and "awareness" programs.

Some years ago, Mr. Paul Vitz undertook a study of American textbooks used in public schools. He found almost no references to religion, even in the context of the formation of our country; in eleventh and twelfth grade history books religion was hardly mentioned, especially in discussing the last seventy to one hundred years. The textbooks also fail to mention the terms marriage, husband, or wife. Instead, a family is defined as a "group of people," frequently without a father, or without children.[7] It is disturbing to think that these are the textbooks that are supposed to introduce students to American society.

On the other hand, the tenets of moral relativism—the idea that there are no real standards, that morality is based on the circumstance, and that each person must decide for himself what is right because there is no outside authority dictating what is right or wrong—are put into the textbooks as truth. Nowhere do the books state that this is simply the viewpoint of certain people.

Instead, young readers are given the distinct impression that this is simply the way the world is. Textbook writers assert that they do not want any "religion" to color their presentation of information, but they color the facts themselves with their own relativistic view of the world.

Humanism, the New Religion

Although the public schools are devoid of any Christian religion, they haven't gotten rid of religion altogether. Instead, the textbooks and goals teach the religion of humanism. When I first heard about secular humanism, as a teacher-in-training at a university, I thought it was nonsense. I didn't see how the philosophy I had learned in school could possibly be called a religion—it didn't even mention God!

That is the point, exactly. Secular humanism doesn't mention God, because there is no living, active God in a humanist philosophy. As the name implies, humans are the controlling factor in the universe. This philosophy has permeated almost every aspect of our society, to the point that you don't even notice it is there until you actively search for it. But it nevertheless affects our children, even if they can't identify it easily.

Humanists believe that man, rather than God, is the measure of all things. They do not recognize God or values relating to him, and believe that each person controls his own destiny. The perfection and goodness of man is assumed. A perusal of Humanist Manifestos I and II reveals other beliefs promoted by humanists:

- All events in history and human development can be explained by evolution.

- The scientific method is applicable to all areas of life and is the only way to find truth.

- All values and beliefs are relative; theology and ideology should have no place in determining ethics; the "situation" is the deciding factor.

- There is no God.

- Man does not have a soul.

- Individualism takes precedence over the community.

- Any type of sexual behavior between consenting adults, euthanasia, and the right to suicide are acceptable.[8]

If you are at all acquainted with secular textbooks or public school curricula, these ideas will seem very familiar to you. In fact, some of them are disseminated daily on television, in newspapers, and through other media. These ideas are accepted as fact, without even an acknowledgment that other perspectives hold them to be false. Many of them are accepted as the norm in the public schools, especially in social studies classes. Subjects such as "values clarification," "death education," and "self-esteem" frequently rely heavily on the tenets of humanism.[9] As humanistic ideas gain popularity in the United States, the teaching of subjects that rely on them for their philosophical underpinnings becomes less subtle.

The secular humanist philosophy is objectionable to many parents. When parents are trying to raise their children to believe in God and his ways and values, it is very frustrating to them—if not downright frightening—to send their children to an institution that teaches them that they can determine their own values and destiny. Since such teaching actively opposes a biblical view of life, the two cannot be reconciled.

The media has covered a variety of disagreements between parents and educators about what type of material should be used with children. Although the media usually portrays these disagreements as "censorship" battles, they are not truly issues of censorship. Webster's Ninth New Collegiate Dictionary defines the verb "to censor" as: "to examine in order to suppress or delete anything considered objectionable." These parents aren't so much trying to suppress the objectionable material as they are trying to insure that their children are taught according to their own values. And this is where the philosophies promulgated in the schools hit home: when they contradict and undermine what parents are attempting to teach their children.

Outcome-Based Education

Outcome-based education (OBE) is another current teaching approach that is radically changing the public schools. By definition, outcome-based education is "any education program that mandates results in terms of a performance . . . The fundamental idea of education oriented toward outcomes is not the problem, but the nature and origin of those outcomes is." [10]

The controversy over outcome-based education does not lie with its principles, but in the outcomes themselves. Not only are they mandated by the federal government, but many of them contain highly questionable goals.

Dr. William Spady is often called the father of OBE, and he says that the outcomes should not be involved with inappropriate emotional and attitudinal goals. But he does believe that the outcomes should include public, or civic goals. When there is a dispute between the family and the school district on a goal, Spady believes the school district should win.[11]

Many people within the educational system disagree about what exactly the objectives should accomplish. And of course, many parents disagree with the majority of the outcomes listed by the government as desirable. For example, one question on a tenth grade language arts test is, "Was there ever a time when you or someone you know felt oppressed or trapped in a relationship? Write briefly about what happened and how the person felt about the oppression." Then the students are supposed to read a story about a woman in an unhappy marriage and decide whether or not the marriage can be saved. The test even provides a section for the student to evaluate his performance.[12]

This sort of test is a problem for many reasons. The first is that knowledge is not what is being tested: there is no specific material that this test is based on. Furthermore, there is no right answer. Each teacher could grade the students according to his or her own personal experience. In addition, spending time on this type of subjective activity takes class time away from the actual reading and writing that should comprise a language arts curriculum. Finally, the subject matter goes beyond what many parents feel is appropriate for classroom study. I, as a parent, would have no interest in having my children's peers decide whether a marriage should be saved: a language arts "test" is simply not the place to be dealing with this complex issue. Many Americans, and most Christians, don't want to believe the schools are teaching these values to their children.

Not only is there ambiguity surrounding the definition of the outcomes, but the standards, many complain, are set so low that they "dummy-down" education. Albert Shanker, president of the American Federation of Teachers, says that many of the standards that are set are "vague and fluffy." [13] And educator Gregory Cizek complains that many of the outcomes are so vague that they could be satisfied with even minimal achievement, and states—with not a little sarcasm—that ". . . we've decided to raise standards so high for 12th graders that we're going to make them pass a 9th grade test in order to get a diploma . . . Over four years, students will get about a dozen tries." [14]

Littleton, Colorado, decided to test the advantages of outcome-based education. The students there were given thirty-six outcomes, or demonstrations, that they were required to perform in order to graduate. The students still took classes and received grades, but the grades had no bearing on whether or not they graduated. As a result, 533 students enrolled in algebra, but only 145 completed the course. 160 students planned to take it for summer school, and the other 228 received incompletes. But since it wasn't a graduation requirement, there was no incentive to finish. The same held true for geometry. Littleton has since dropped its OBE graduation outcomes, and returned to the more traditional standards. [15]

How ironic that the entire country is now being told to adopt a program that has already failed in the areas where it has been tried. Not only does OBE have useless outcomes, it lowers standards that don't need to be lowered any further. OBE is filled with trouble, and many parents do not want their children to be part of it.

Goals 2000: Whose Goals?

Another troublesome matter is the legislation passed in March 1994 by the U.S. Congress. Introduced as House Bill HR6 and now termed Goals 2000, it was one of the biggest and most comprehensive bills on education ever to be introduced to the Congress. Ostensibly designed to be an overhaul of public education, in reality it is an incredibly huge governmental intervention into many areas of school management and family life, and many believe it is the most damaging piece of legislation to be passed in recent years.

Basically, Goals 2000 dictates how schools will be run and what they will teach. Though its mandates are "voluntary," schools would lose significant amounts of funding if they declined the government's offer. Furthermore, it creates an entirely new bureaucracy in Washington, D. C., to supposedly handle local schools.

Comments from those involved in the battle when the bill was before Congress indicate their awareness of the dangers of the legislation.

Senator Malcolm Wallop, R-Wyo., for instance, accurately described the intrusiveness of the federal government as he denounced the bill:

> Like virtually every other sector in this country which the federal government touches, the educational structure is flabby from federal pork . . . And here we are talking about giving the government even more control over the basic education programs for our children. This bill is yet another step in the federal government's takeover of education in general.[16]

Journalist Cal Thomas, calling Goals 2000 the "dumbing down of a generation," wrote: "How should parents respond to this latest government power grab? Just as they would if they knew their children's school was on fire—they should get them out, fast."[17]

The heart of Goals 2000 is a set of national educational goals, many of which sound very reasonable to the unsuspecting public, e.g., "The high-school graduation rate will increase to at least 90 percent," and "U.S. students will be first in the world in science and math achievements." Other goals center around literacy, drug-free classrooms, and parent participation. Although this rhetoric sounds innocent enough, it is the means by which these ideals are to be achieved that threatens family units and parental responsibility in the home. Cathy Duffy, in her book *Government Nannies*, says:

> At first glance, these goals might sound reasonable. And, if pursued by private means and voluntary programs, some of them might even be praiseworthy. However, Goals 2000, backed by related legislation, aims to expand government-as-nanny programs much more, and all attempts at subtlety are likely to disappear. The "partnership" is shaping up to be an invasion.[18]

For example, the first goal is that all children will start school "ready to learn." This sounds like a great idea, but how will it be accomplished? Unfortunately, it becomes an excuse to monitor and intrude on families with young children, seeking to "help" them with programs and interventions. It becomes downright frightening when that single goal is used as an excuse to invade thousands of homes and undermine the actions of the parents.

Schools thus are in the business of "fixing" families, rather than teaching academics. There is only so much time in a school day, so academic subjects will get a smaller portion of time, to allow time for these other goals.[19]

The goal that all children will start school ready to learn was the rationale for such programs as Head Start, which was designed for kids that are "high risk." Unfortunately, in the Goals 2000 (and other) legislation, the definition of "high risk" has been so expanded that the door has been opened wide for government intervention into the lives of nearly any American family. The more inclusive definition would allow almost any child to be labeled "at risk." For example, according to the Missouri Department of Education, a child can be "at risk" if it appears to a social worker that the parent does not exhibit a "caring attitude," or does not understand a baby's cues. A family is considered "at risk" if it is undergoing stress, which can be defined as divorce, a parent that travels regularly, the birth of a new baby, or the prolonged illness of a family member. Still other factors that will put a child into the "at risk" category are allergies, a parent that smokes heavily, too few toys, or a "lack of routine" in the home.[20]

Clearly, these guidelines would allow any family to be classified as "at risk," and therefore a candidate for government intervention. How many families do not have one or more of these circumstances or situations in their homes at one time or another? Thus, your grandchildren could be labeled "at-risk" by the government, because they have moved recently, or because they don't "connect" with each other! This is sobering, as determining who should be forced into the programs is obviously a subjective decision.

Once a child has been labeled "at risk," he is then vulnerable to the invasion, visits, and documentation that are standard operating procedures for a social worker when dealing with abuse cases. From there, the programs and monitoring will begin. The law mandates the use of a survey called "The National Household Education Survey" to begin this process, which queries children on various activities that go on in their own homes. This program violates personal freedoms, ostensibly to insure that a few needy children get the programs they need. But since it isn't always easy to tell who needs the help, all children will be forced into the system, for, as the bill states, " . . . some irresponsible families need help to do what is right for their children, so we will require all families to raise their children according to our guidelines." [21]

The public schools will be plagued by these policies, and the government will use them to glean information about each family. And what I have discussed of the agenda of Goals 2000 is only the tip of the iceberg.

Dr. James Dobson, noted psychologist and author, summarized some of the more troublesome portions of the Goals 2000 legislation in his newsletter of May 1994, including the following three aspects of the law: control of local schools taken out of parents' hands and co-opted by the federal government; the mandate for outcome-based education; and the creation of even more bureaucracies at the federal level.

He explained that one goal of the National Educational Association (NEA) is to control the education of all children. (The NEA is a long-time supporter of such anti-family causes as homosexual activism, abortion, and "condom-mania." Their organization is having some success in undermining the influence of parents.)

He warned readers that the bill fully supports outcome-based education, emphasizing learning outcomes such as "problem-solving," "effective communication," and "appreciating others"—terms that do not represent any actual knowledge gained or skills learned. (Even organizations such as the National Right to Read

Foundation were dismayed at the manner in which this legislation would affect children's learning.)

Moreover, the legislation also states that learning basic skills is not necessary in order to understand more complex ideas, and instructs the schools to teach "content-rich" material instead. This kind of instruction is the opposite of traditional education, which teaches basic reading and writing skills before anything else.

Robert Sweet, former director of the National Institute of Education, reports that, as a result of this new philosophy of education, standardized tests will no longer measure academic achievement in content areas. The test scores will actually go up, however, because the tests will be dummied down, thus "proving" that the new methods are working. Educational content will have gone out of style, in favor of "process and reasoning" skills.

Many other commentators and educators are pleading the same case, and trying to head off the new agenda before it is completely entrenched in the schools. Until the Goals 2000 legislation is reversed, however, the education of most children will be increasingly controlled at the federal level, leaving almost no discretionary control in the hands of the parents or the local school board.[22]

Does More Money Equal Better Schools?

The ironic part of all this is that statistics do not support the argument that more money improves education. Money has been poured into the public education system in recent years, but test scores, school safety, and student achievement have continued on a downward trend. So even though most schools will accept the Goals 2000 money and agenda, it is unlikely that they will see any improvement in test scores or behavior, and may actually see a further decrease.

The Spring 1995 issue of *The Home School Court Report* contained an article about the federal role in education and its detrimental effects, in which the writer stated:

> American student performance may be down, but spending is up. Way up. Do not be led astray by thinking, "Of course spending is up for education. The cost of everything is up since the 1960's or 1970's because of inflation." All figures on educational spending contained in the following paragraphs have been adjusted for inflation, so a true comparison can be made in real 1994 dollars.
>
> In the 1972-73 school year, the per pupil cost for elementary and secondary education was $3,393 (adjusted for inflation, stated in 1994 dollars). In 1993-94, America spent $5,313 per pupil—an increase of 56.6% in real spending . . .
>
> The sad reality is that the pattern which has emerged from the federal role in education is a pattern of more spending (especially for administration), fewer students, lower SAT scores, lower graduation rates, and dismal rates of academic proficiency.[23]

Though more and more money is poured into public education, the results have not been positive. At some point the administrators and decision-makers will realize this, but it will be difficult to turn the situation around. In the meantime, many students will struggle with and be frustrated by the system.

Can the Public Schools Be Saved?

Unfortunately, the problems I have outlined could take years to correct—at the expense of many children—if they are ever corrected at all. The speech made by John Taylor Gatto in 1990 upon receiving the "New York City

Teacher of the Year" award is revealing. He said of the public schools:

> The daily misery around us is, I think, in large measure caused by the fact that, as Paul Goodman put it thirty years ago, we force children to grow up absurd. Any reform in schooling has to deal with its absurdities.
>
> It is absurd and anti-life to be part of a system that compels you to sit in confinement with people of exactly the same age and social class. That system effectively cuts you off from the immense diversity of life and the synergy of variety; indeed it cuts you off from your own past and future, sealing you in a continuous present much the same way television does . . .
>
> Two institutions at present control our children's lives: television and schooling, in that order; both of these reduce the real world of wisdom, fortitude, temperance, and justice to a never-ending, non-stop abstraction. In centuries past, the time of the child and adolescent would be spent in real work, real charity, real adventures, and the realistic search for mentors who might teach what you really wanted to learn. A great deal of time was spent in community pursuits, practicing affection, meeting and studying every level of the community, learning how to make a home, and dozens of other tasks necessary to become a whole man or a whole woman.[24]

Homeschooling: A Viable Alternative

Hopefully, homeschooled kids can avoid all of this. Homeschooled children all over the country have the opportunity to learn and grow—without the trappings of a public school system, and with the expenditure of far fewer dollars. Even more importantly, they will have a moral and ethical upbringing that is contrary and far superior to what public school teachers are told to teach their students.

Although many parents begin homeschooling because of problems in the public schools, most would not go back to public school even if the schools were miraculously healed of their problems. Not only have they begun to reap the academic rewards of schooling their children at home, but they have begun to see positive changes in their life together as a family.

Chapter 2
....

Why Homeschool?
Building a Strong Family

HOW GOOD AND PLEASANT IT IS WHEN
BROTHERS LIVE TOGETHER IN UNITY! —PSALM 133:1

Hlow long does your sister plan to homeschool her children?" I asked a friend whose sister had been homeschooling for several years. I was not yet homeschooling,
and was still skeptical of the concept.

"I don't know," she replied, shaking her head. "She
says she'll do it for as long as she and her kids enjoy it."

This was the strangest answer to that question I had
yet heard.

* * * * *

The fact is that many people continue to homeschool long beyond their intended "stopping point"
because of the positive changes they see in their families.
Their children are happier, and relationships among siblings and between children and parents are stronger
because of the time they all spend at home together.

Our modern culture does little to bond families

together. Children spend much of their day in school, and come home to a different set of rules and circumstances. In school they were expected to listen to and respect their teachers; they must now transfer that respect and obedience to their mother. On the other hand, their mother may not even be home, and they may either stay at home alone or go to some day care facility until their mother arrives in the evening after working all day. Each person comes home with his own set of experiences and emotions, and frequently has difficulty meshing with the family at the end of the day. Many parents find themselves looking forward to seeing their children off to school the next day, because they don't feel they have much control over them, and they don't share many common experiences.

The following scenario—which my children and I witnessed recently—is a good example of this disaffection between family members of today. The children and I were in the locker room at the local pool getting dried and dressed after swimming lessons. Also in the locker room were a mother and her teenage daughter.

The daughter sat on a bench with a towel wrapped around her, complaining that she was too cold to get dressed. As the mother was dressing, she constantly urged her daughter to get moving. Finally she threatened:

"If you don't get dressed, I won't take you to Wal-mart."

"Yes, you will. I want to go," responded the daughter.

"Well you won't, if you don't hurry. Come on, put on some clothes."

"I can't. I'm cold. You're just a witch." She giggled. "A witch with a W."

Her mom didn't even flinch. "Well you're a brat with a B. Here's your shoe. Hey, what's in this shoe? Look, it's full of rocks."

The daughter giggled again, and reached for the

shoe. Putting her hand into it, she pulled out a pebble and threw it at her mom.

"Hey, cut it out! Now get dressed."

Instead, the daughter continued to throw little rocks at her mom, while her mother repeated her threats to skip going to Wal-Mart.

I tried to dress my little ones quickly, as they were dumfounded at the scene before them. By the time we left, the daughter had run out of rocks but still had made no effort to put her clothes on.

Later that evening, my seven-year-old turned to me. "Mom, why did those people in the locker room talk to each other that way?" she asked.

My second-born is extremely sensitive, and her voice was full of hurt when she asked the question. I told her that some families are like that, and asked her if she wasn't glad that in our family we don't treat each other that way? Although I could have spoken my mind about how what we witnessed is a result of not disciplining children when they are young, I didn't need to. My kids had a vivid reminder of how pleasant—by comparison—their home life is.

Homeschooling family interactions are usually much different from what was was apparently a fairly typical exchange for this mother and daughter. I am not saying that those who don't homeschool their kids will have this kind of negative home atmosphere, but homeschooling does allow parents many more opportunities to create a positive home environment than do other educational options.

The Lost Art of Togetherness

A day for a homeschooling family is radically different

from a typical American's weekday. Because the mother is with her children all day, she learns to discipline and motivate her children according to what is best for their particular temperaments. She finds out where they are weak, and where they are strong. She learns to deal with problem areas and work on them with each child.

In addition, all are working towards common goals. Family members do projects together, go on field trips, and participate in community service. They learn to function as a group, not just a bunch of individuals who live under the same roof. The pastor of my former church has described what he calls the "boarding house family." In this kind of family, each member has his own activities, his own goals, and his own friends. Possibly they eat dinner together. Most of the time, they all sleep there. But that's all. The typical American family has begun to look more and more like this model, but homeschoolers have rejected it. They know there is a better way to live.

A homeschooling family has large blocks of time in which to develop relationships, and spends far more hours together than does the typical American family. These hours are used to knit a strong family unit. They are also hours that require siblings who spend almost every waking moment together to learn to get along.

I have met people who say that their children cannot spend more than half of an hour together before they have to be separated, and most of us, in fact, are accustomed to the idea that many brothers and sisters dislike each other. This situation can be magnified in a homeschool setting, where spending time together is unavoidable. This may be a struggle for homeschool families, but they have to work on a solution. Homeschool mothers use Scriptures, discipline, and creative arrangements of time and areas to help children learn to work together.

Although there is certainly some effort involved for the kids as well as the parents, the results are worth it. A child who can learn to get along with his siblings as well as care for them and help them, can probably learn to get along with anyone. Children have a tendency to be much kinder to kids they don't see very often than they are to their siblings. So once brothers and sisters have learned to compromise and learn together, they have learned skills that will last them a lifetime.

Homeschooling families also learn through the struggles of family life. Adversity can build character in ourselves, our children, and our families. When a difficult situation arises in a family, the family must come together to meet the challenge, rather than break apart. Homeschooling families are required to work through their troubles together, and thus they build confidence in themselves and their strength as a family.

A recent issue of *The Teaching Home* included a letter from a woman sharing her family's experience with the children's grandfather when he was dying of cancer. She said they were able to spend his final days at his side—simply bringing their school books along with them.[1] Thus the family was able to bond together at this critical time, and the children were able to participate in an experience that will remain with them all their lives.

A Flexible Schedule

Homeschooling allows you to be remarkably efficient in the use of time. We begin our day at nine A.M. The girls feed the rabbits and the dog, and make sure they have made their beds and cleaned their rooms. At nine-thirty we begin with a Bible time, and then move into the academic subjects. Occasionally we will get sidetracked and use some extra time, but for the most part we move steadily through math, reading, language, spelling, history and science. Each of the children does the same number of math pages every day, but the amount of history they do varies greatly. At the beginning of a unit my fourth grader will read the entire history chapter, which would probably take a child in a classroom several days to cover. As a result, we cover a lot a material in a small amount of time. We are almost always finished with our school work by one o' clock.

As children reach the junior and senior high grades, they frequently have to work an hour or two into the afternoon to finish their assignments, but not any later than that. This provides a unique situation for families. Children have completed the formal learning desired, but only half of the day is gone. That extra time opens up a whole world of possibilities.

Unique Learning Opportunities

Some families use that period of time to train their older children in a trade or homemaking skills. A few afternoons a week can be spent with the father learning his trade. On other afternoons, the mother can give lessons in sewing, baking, cleaning, or knitting. The possibilities are almost endless for a child who is trained to use this time to learn new things and expand his experiences.

I know of two homeschool families whose children help at a veterinary clinic a couple of mornings a week. I talked with the vet about this arrangement, and he said it was wonderful for him as well as the kids. He mentioned that kids in public schools could only help out after four in the afternoon, and that there wasn't much for them to do at that time. All of his surgery and work with the animals was done in the morning. So these homeschooled

kids have arranged their school time around the veteri-
narian's hours, in order to spend time with him when he
needs them the most and while he is doing the procedures
that teach them the most. He likes having the help, and
they learn a tremendous amount about the world of veterinary care.

In larger cities, homeschoolers have many activities
they can participate in when their schoolwork is over,
including basketball teams, soccer teams, art classes,
choir groups, and science clubs. As the number of homeschoolers grows, so do the available activities.

Rickey Boyer, the son of Marilyn and Rick Boyer, is
a young man whose homeschool schedule gave him the
time to actively pursue his interest in politics. Describing
Rickey's achievements, his father says:

> My eldest son was elected chairman of our coun-
> ty's Republican party at the age of nineteen. That was a
> milestone in his political activity, but not the beginning
> of it. He traces his interest back to the presidential elec-
> tion of 1980 when he was six years old. I mentioned to
> the family one evening that I was about to walk down to
> the neighbor's house for a few minutes to catch the TV
> news about the election (we have never had a televi-
> sion). My sons asked me who the good guy was and I told
> them that I favored Reagan over Carter, thus making
> Reagan a hero at our house regardless of the fact that
> none of the children knew the first thing about him.
> Rickey had already demonstrated a strong interest in his-
> tory and government, having read . . .[a] fourth grade
> history book cover to cover eight times before the end of
> first grade. From that time on he read history books,
> newspapers and political magazines as fast as he could get
> his hands on them. This led to working as a volunteer in
> local elections when he was still so young he had to hitch
> a ride to headquarters for lack of a driver's license. Now
> twenty, he has seen his interest in politics spread to his

brothers and sisters as well as a number of friends . . .
There's a lot of difference between the way I learned
about government and the way they did it. I learned it in
a classroom, isolated from the real thing. They learned
about it in the process of doing the job.[2]

Avoiding Student Burn-Out

The most important benefit of the way homeschooled
students' days are structured is decreased burn-out. Kids
who spend six hours a day, five days a week in a school
building usually suffer some degree of frustration, restless-
ness, or boredom. But kids who have the time to pursue
the variety of the interests and activities that are available to homeschoolers do not experience boredom or
frustration. They are involved in group activities, or an
in-depth project, or an area of service, and the burn-out
rate is much lower. Also, since the time spent in a formal
learning situation is so much less, and so concentrated,
most kids don't end up hating their school work the way
public school kids often do.

That's not to say that they are always enthusiastic
about doing their work: they are still children. But they
have a greater variety of choices, and this can make all
the difference in turning around negative attitudes. For
instance, in recent weeks, my children have been on an
all-day field trip to Fort Laramie and Bridger Cliffs, a field
trip to the Botanical Gardens, gone swimming three
times, attended Sunday school and a church kid's group,
been to two birthday parties, played with three different
families in the evening, delivered a May Day flower, had
piano and art lessons, decorated cakes, and cut out
numerous paper dolls.

54

Are They Missing Out?

Although some people object that homeschooled kids "miss out" on many things, I see it quite differently. Yes, there are some situations that cannot be duplicated at home and therefore will not be experienced by a home-schooled child. School parties and playing on the school playground, for example, are not a part of the home-school experience. Also, there are more social experiences built into the school activities in the upper grades. On the other hand, many communities now allow home-schooled children to participate in athletic events and other extra-curricular activities. In addition, Christian schools usually welcome homeschoolers to participate in certain activities, such as school pictures, field days, and art lessons.

In any case, from my perspective, it is the public school children who are missing out on so much. Take field trips, for example. When I was a child, a field trip meant we rode on a large, noisy bus for a long time. Then we were herded through a museum or tour of something, usually led by a tour guide that we barely listened to. We ate a brown bag lunch and then rode the bus back to school. Though I remembered much of what I saw, I didn't very often apply it to anything we had done in the classroom. My biggest feeling was usually that of amazement that so much went on in the world while I was in school. The most educational part for me was watching the day-to-day activities beyond the classroom.

Field Trips, Homeschool-Style

Now when I go on a field trip with my children or another group of homeschoolers, I can see how much I missed as a child. We all get to drive together in the family car, which has great advantages over a school bus. Field trips taken with the whole family are also more interesting, since each child is at a different age and stage of development.

Often we can go through the exhibits at our own pace, focusing on those we have studied the most or that interest the children the most. Though we sometimes have to stand aside for a few minutes while a public school group comes through, the rest of the time we have as much time as we would like in each place. Best of all, we can all interact with one another about what we are seeing. The kids ask questions, I explain how something ties in with a subject we are studying or a book they have read, and their experience widens. They can ask questions or sort through a new thought out loud, and we all learn from it. The educational value of even a simple field trip is greatly expanded because of the one-on-one follow-through I can give—follow-through that would be difficult with a large group.

Even a trip to the grocery store can become an educational experience. Last week, while shopping, my seven-year old asked:

"Mommy, since everyone has to have food to live, why do grocery stores try to make money? Why can't they give the food away?"

I explained to her the basic economics of the costs involved in putting one item on the shelf, and how each of the people at the store had to make money in order to live. As we were walking down the aisles, I noticed one of the young employees walking with us. When we turned the corner he grinned sheepishly at me and said, "I want to hear this too!"

Though he went on with his work, I noticed that I kept "running into him." I guess seeing a mother explain basic economics to a youngster is an unusual sight.

I am thankful to be there for my children's questions and to pique their curiosity during the day. After all, satisfying curiosity is the best motivation for learning.

Off-Season Vacations

Another advantage of the homeschool schedule is the opportunity to take off-season vacations. This is a wonderful bonus, both for fun and for learning. One year our family went to Indiana in October to see the brilliant fall foliage. We stayed in a cabin in a state park while the weather was cool and sunny, instead of hot and humid as it would have been in the summer. My children brought home bags full of nuts, seeds, and other treasures that they had never seen in our dry, arid Wyoming climate. They went to an Amish farm and rode in a carriage, watched apple cider being made and a blacksmith at work. Though we could have done these things in the summer, we would have faced crowds and heat.

Next May we are planning to visit the Mesa Verde Indian ruins in Colorado. This will be a great chance for the kids to see firsthand how the Native Americans lived, and the crowds will be much smaller. The opportunities are endless when you drop the restriction of having to travel between the months of June and August. Many employers appreciate it too, because you aren't trying to get time off when everyone else is.

The Family Business

Many homeschooling families have built family businesses with their available time and resources. This is probably the ultimate family project. At the very least, the children learn skills and develop talents that can be used for a lifetime. Many of these children go on to take over the business when their parents retire, thereby giving them a lifelong occupation independent of an employer. Parents apprentice their children, and the business grows to support the family.

One such family is the Barth family, a family that travels together giving seminars on homeschooling, and selling their tape "The Blessings of Homeschooling." Each family member—parents as well as children—gives a brief testimony about how homeschooling has benefited him, and what he has gained as a result. As teenagers, the two oldest sons were able to spend their afternoons in their father's shop learning to make dental appliances. They now run their own dental appliance business. In addition to helping with the household duties and learning home-making skills, the daughters have handled the mail orders for the tape business as well as secretarial work for their father. All of the children have taught themselves to play a musical instrument. The eighteen-year-old plays the harp and builds antique reproduction furniture—skills he learned on his own. The Barth children were able to learn and develop these skills because as homeschoolers there were large blocks of time available to them, and also because they developed discipline and possessed teachable spirits—the fruit of growing up in a godly home.[3]

Writing in *The Teaching Home*, one mother summa-rized the ways in which her family had benefited since beginning homeschooling several years ago. She reported that homeschooling has become a lifestyle—a way of life—rather than just a style of education. She listed five areas in which she and her husband feel positive changes have been made since the children have been home all day:

- Spiritual health: they can make God's Word a vital part of their children's lives.

- Physical health: their kids bring home fewer illnesses and have less stress.

- Discipline: they are able to instill their own values in a consistent manner.

- Socialization: they like to teach their children to love God and love others, and they can teach respect in an active way.

- Family unity: they are pleased to know and understand their children better, since they have begun to spend so much time with them. They have built strong relationships with their children.[4]

It is apparent that the benefits of homeschooling go much farther and deeper than academic achievement, as important as that is. As your grandchildren grow and thrive through homeschooling, you will begin to keep your own list of ways you have reaped the rewards of your children's decision to follow a path less traveled, direct their children's education at home, and build a strong family life. You will no doubt also begin to see changes in the spiritual lives of your grandchildren, for your children have an unparalleled opportunity to teach your grandchildren in this important aspect of their lives as well.

Chapter Three
· · · · · · · · · · · · · · · · · · · ·

Why Homeschool?
Biblical Mandate

TRAIN A CHILD IN THE WAY HE SHOULD GO, AND
WHEN HE IS OLD HE WILL NOT TURN FROM IT.
—PROVERBS 22:6

Mommy, how does God work in our hearts?"

"What is more important to God, making dresses for our Christmas play or writing your book?"

"Did Jesus have to learn contentment on the cross?"

"Hey, Mom, the snow stopped! Do you know why? A little girl was having trouble being good and he stopped making it snow to help her."

"Where was our furniture when God was making us?"

These are just a few of the questions my girls have flung my way at times I was not expecting them. Only one of them was asked during a devotion or teaching time— the rest were just out-of-the-blue thoughts that popped up while we were doing other things.

* * * *

Living with and teaching children every hour they are awake offers parents a unique chance to develop their children's faith, and may be the best motivation for any family to teach their children at home. Those who choose to homeschool believe that being around for questions like those I listed—and giving children the biblical foundation to launch such questions—is the most important job they will ever have. In fact, although a number of factors may lead to the decision to teach children at home, many families simply feel that God has led them in this direction. They report that prayer and conviction as a result of reading God's Word were the primary factors in their decision to homeschool.

In my research with homeschool families, I found that while many expressed disappointment over their parents' (often very vocal) disapproval of homeschooling, and considered it to be a definite drawback to their choice to homeschool, all but one said they would still homeschool, regardless of their parents' reactions, because they knew that it was what God wanted them to do.

I remember a conversation I had several years ago— before my kids were school age—with a friend who had begun homeschooling. When I asked her why she had decided to do it, she shrugged, and said, "God told me to."

Noticing my puzzled look, she continued, "He told me to do it, and then later he told my husband to do it. So that's what we have done."

She made it sound so simple! But she was obviously certain of her choice.

Using the Bible for guidance in making such decisions may not come naturally for many parents, and some may find it difficult to get specific direction from the pages of Scripture. But ever-increasing numbers of parents are finding not only guidance in Scripture, but teachings and instructions for the raising of their children. The Old and New Testaments contain many references to the responsibilities that parents have in the education of their children.

Whose Responsibility Is It?

To most people, Christian or not, the idea of letting God decide how your children will be educated is a foreign one. For several decades, people have routinely sent their children off to public school without a second thought. It has only been recently that such a course has been questioned.

Much of the argument about how and where children should be educated revolves around the subject of responsibility. Who is responsible for the education of the children? Over the years, the public school system has come to believe that *it* is responsible, that it, in effect, has ownership of the children in the United States.

Horace Mann, considered to be the "father of public education," had a lot to do with the public acceptance of that belief. Mann believed that we could create a better world through public education. He believed that the public school should become for modern man what the church was for the medieval man. He believed that public schools established according to his vision would produce citizens that were morally and intellectually superior to their forefathers.

Mann taught that in order to create the ideal society, the masses must be manipulated by society's elite into conforming to these new ideals. According to him, the state, rather than the parents, knows what is best for the children. Public education controlled by advocates of Mann's philosophy would be devoid of any religious teaching.[1]

Horace Mann and other educators also promoted the notion that children are better off taught by someone other than their own parents, and that is the accepted belief today.

Homeschooling parents have a different view of the matter. They believe that they, and they alone, have the responsibility for teaching and training their children, and they have decided that, given their options, the best place to do that is at home.

Spiritual Training

Beyond the academics, by teaching their children at home, parents are in the best possible position to teach them about spiritual matters. This is a tremendous responsibility, but one that they feel they must undertake themselves. They know that God will help them in their endeavor and will bless their efforts when they follow him.

They take seriously the biblical mandate in Deuteronomy 6:5-7 to "Love the Lord your God with all your heart and with all your strength. These commandments . . . are to be upon your hearts. Impress them on your children. Talk about them when you sit at home and when you walk along the road, when you lie down and when you get up." This is a beautiful illustration of the all-encompassing way we are to teach our children—by incorporating our teaching into everything we do with them. Most school children are away from eight in the morning (or earlier!) until four in the afternoon, and after that are busy with sports, other extra-curricular activities, or homework. There is very little time left in which to talk to them of spiritual matters. It's hard to instruct your children "when you sit at home and when you walk along the road, when you lie down and when you get up," if they are off at school! Consequently, parents choose to homeschool so that their children can be home with them during the day, enabling them to incorporate God's views and principles into their daily lives.

Raising Godly Children

For most homeschool families, teaching children biblical principles is done in two ways. The first is the casual approach, as the verse above implies. Parents learn to talk with their children during even the most mundane tasks, teaching them spiritual truths throughout the day. The beauty of this approach is in its spontaneity. My children come up with the most profound questions at unpredictable times. Serving cottage cheese for lunch becomes the occasion for a discussion of which foods come from God, and which foods man makes. Helping a woman at the grocery store is a chance to teach respect for older people. Parents that spend the vast majority of their time with their children have unlimited opportunities of these kinds.

The second method is more planned. Most homeschoolers have a course in the Bible as the first, and frequently the longest, period of the day. Children are taught to read the Bible and to understand it. They write about it, discuss it, and apply it. Though the Bible is the basis of these studies, they can also include books by great Christian writers, Bible handbooks, commentaries, and other Bible study material. Whatever method is used, students get intensive Bible training that will benefit them throughout their lives.

For example, my daughter recently heard a song on a Christian radio station that she didn't quite understand. Knowing that the song came from Scripture, I was able to show her how to use a concordance and find the verse for herself. She was delighted to find that the song had, indeed, quoted the verse correctly, and she wrote it on a piece of paper to hang on her wall. It is important to me that my children are so comfortable with the Bible that this type of response happens frequently.

Discipleship

Along with teaching comes the opportunity to disciple the children. Matthew 28:19 tells us to "go and make disciples of all nations, baptizing them in the name of the Father and of the Son and of the Holy Spirit, and teaching them to obey everything I have commanded you." This verse instructs us to make disciples, and that begins at home.

Although all Christian parents can lead their children to a saving knowledge of Jesus Christ, homeschool parents are ideally suited for it, because they have taken complete responsibility for their children's training.

As a mother teaches her children daily, she can help them understand the verses that explain the process of salvation. Romans 10:9 is one of the clearest: "If you confess with your mouth, 'Jesus is Lord,' and believe in your heart that God raised him from the dead, you will be saved." In this way, a parent can explain that in order to receive eternal life, as well as an abundant life on earth, a person must admit he is separated from God and receive Jesus as his Savior in order to eliminate that separation. Similarly, many of the verses and parables in Scriptures are easily understood and applied by children.

When my older two children were at the age to understand these verses, I was negligent in teaching them. I had no idea that I could have been—and should have been—teaching them these principles myself. So I let a Bible school teacher lay the groundwork. I regret that now, as I have come to realize that I am fully capable of laying the groundwork myself—and much more enthusiastic about my children than any Bible teacher. I am now teaching my younger two children the principles they need to know to enter the kingdom of God.

The second half of Matthew 28:19 is that of teaching disciples to obey all of God's Word. This is the second step that homeschooled parents can take with their children, as they teach them extensively about the Bible and all that God has for those who will follow him.

Bible-Based Curricula

In addition to these methods, a family's curriculum choices can add to the training process as well. Most homeschool curricula are biblically based, and therefore teach that God is related to every situation in which we find ourselves. For example, one third grade science text contains sections entitled God Gave Us Water, God Promises to Protect His Creation, God Gave Us Heat and Cold, God Cares for Man, and God Told Man to Care for His Creation, etc. The framework for the book is God's design and the subjects (the physical sciences, animal studies, health) are all studied in relation to that central theme.

Christian history texts offer another example of the strong Christian emphasis homeschools can maintain. One third grade history book is comprised completely of biographies. Some of the people studied are John Greenleaf Whittier, Noah Webster, Abraham Lincoln, and Robert E. Lee. Instead of requiring the students to just memorize dates and a few accomplishments, this book delves into the personal and spiritual life of each person. Abraham Lincoln and George Washington were both strong Christians raised in Christian homes. Noah

Webster became a Christian as an adult, after intense Bible reading, and shortly after that began writing the first dictionary, which took almost twenty years.[2] These essential facts are left out of secular texts.

By reading about these Americans in a Christian textbook, children can see how God uses people to shape the world—a much richer and more accurate way of studying the core subjects. Texts such as these can increase the Christian atmosphere in a home, and help fulfill the scriptural mandates—a task not easily accomplished when the children are in public school.

It may be argued that a Christian school can also do all this. While it is true that a Christian school can use a biblical curriculum, it is unlikely that a teacher responsible for a large group of students can individually instruct each child in the ways of God, or bring him to a saving knowledge of Jesus Christ.

A parent is the best person to design a child's spiritual training. Only a parent knows the child's specific character strengths and weaknesses. Only a parent knows what areas her child struggles with. The parent is therefore in the best position to teach the child as the verse commands. The constant togetherness that homeschooling provides is the ideal atmosphere to carry out the instruction of children in God's ways.

The concept of apprenticeship illustrates this principle well. For example, a journeyman bricklayer begins the job of laying bricks without knowing anything about his craft. At the outset, he is assigned to, and works alongside of, an experienced bricklayer. First, they choose the right bricks, ones that are the right shape and in good condition. They want to build a wall that will be strong, nice-looking, and long-lasting. Next, the bricklayer mixes up the mortar. Only the finest materials go into the mortar, and they must be measured out in exactly the right proportions. Though there is a formula the bricklayer follows, he uses his own judgment to determine when the solution is just right. Finally, they begin to lay the bricks and spread the mortar between the cracks. The right amount must be put on each joint, and all the joints must be even; otherwise, the wall will lean and eventually topple. The apprentice watches the process, takes it in, and tries it himself. He gets tips and ideas from his teacher, gradually becoming more skillful. The master bricklayer guides him every step of the way. Eventually, he becomes skilled enough to work on his own, possibly even surpassing his teacher in skill.

This analogy has many parallels to homeschooling. We, as parents, are the senior bricklayers, and we want to teach our children to do well. What better way to teach them than to guide them step-by-step, to constantly train them up in the ways of the Lord, with the goal of raising godly men and women to influence the world? We must teach carefully, so the work we do will endure, and last many years. We do not want our work to topple and crumble when the first wind blows. We must teach to the best of our ability, and keep our sights on the goal of raising godly children.

When God calls families to this task, they can expect to be rewarded for their efforts.

Chapter Four

. . . .

What About Socialization?

HE WHO WALKS WITH THE WISE GROWS WISE,
BUT A COMPANION OF FOOLS SUFFERS HARM.
—PROVERBS 13:20

[WHEN] MY NIECE STARTED HOMESCHOOLING . . .
I DID WONDER ABOUT THE SOCIAL GRACES HER CHILD
MIGHT HAVE . . . BUT TIME PASSED AND . . . THE
CHILDREN ALL SEEMED PERFECTLY NORMAL TO ME . . .[1]
—POLLY GILPIN

When their children began homeschooling, Polly
Gilpin and Dorothy Ferguson, the two grandparents
introduced at the beginning of the book, had the usual
questions about socialization. Polly was afraid the children would be "in-grown," and not able to handle every-
day interactions. She says that she was originally afraid
that homeschooled students wouldn't be able to cope
with the real world.

It wasn't until Dorothy saw her grandson playing a
musical instrument in front of hundreds of people that
she realized he was actually "socializing" just fine. In time,
both women began to see that homeschooled kids were

better able to cope with the real world than many public-schooled children.

Many grandparents fear their children will be social misfits if taught at home. If the children are older, grandma sometimes worries that they will be inept in groups at church, and tongue-tied with other children, incapable of building a relationship with anyone outside the home. In fact, the opposite is true. Though socialization is probably the most frequently voiced fear about homeschooling, it is an easy issue to address.

Webster's Ninth New Collegiate Dictionary defines the word "socialize" thus: "to make social; esp.: to fit or train for a social environment." Most people would agree that socialization means teaching children to get along with others. Unfortunately, most people also agree that the best way to do that is to put a child in with his peers when he is five, and let the group train him. This method has serious flaws.

Modeling

Consider a new mother with a soon-to-be toddler. Sitting down on the floor, she smiles at her little son, who is hanging onto the couch and teetering on his little feet. She puts her arms in front of her, coaxing.

"Come here, James. Come to Mommy! You can do it!"

He waddles first one, then two, then three steps, and falls into her open arms.

Tears filling her eyes, she swoops him up. "Yes! You walked to Mommy! You took your first steps. Oh honey, you are growing up so fast!"

James learns to walk by watching those around him. He studies Mom and Dad putting one foot in front of the other, and eventually he experiments himself.

Through a process of imitating and being encouraged, he takes his first halting, wobbly steps, gradually improving until he is not only walking, but skipping and running with ease.

As parents, we are instrumental in the implementation of this process for all the major milestones of a youngster's life until he is about five years old. We know that our child will learn to walk, talk, eat, drink, interact, and function according to the model that we set before him from birth. But when he turns five years old, suddenly we see ourselves as inadequate. We think he now needs a "professional" to do what we have been doing successfully for the past five years.

While there are some skills that we may not feel educated or prepared enough to teach our children, how to interact socially should not be one of them. Since we have been functioning in a social world for our entire adult lives, why do we see ourselves as incapable of passing on that knowledge to our children? We are the best teachers our children could have in this area, certainly superior to a group of kids whose values and behaviors are unfamiliar to us. Social skills can be—and are—easily practiced in a home environment. Most importantly, at home it is the parent who determines just what these skills will be.

If you put a five-year-old in the middle of a group of five-year-olds, who does he learn from? He is most likely not going to pattern his behavior after the adult, though she is his best example of socialization. Instead, he is going to imitate what he sees the other children do. Thus begins a habit of learning from other children instead of from adults—a habit that is turning out to be grossly harmful to many of our nation's children.

Once at a homeschool conference I went to a workshop led by Jonathan Lindvall, a homeschool speaker and ex-public school teacher who has homeschooled his own children for several years. He reported that parents often came to him saying things like "I am so glad you are my child's teacher. I know he will learn a lot under you." He said his consistent response was, "Thank you for your confidence, but there is only one of me, and there are thirty other students. Your child will learn a lot more from them than he will from me."

Walking with the Wise

A popular homeschool magazine recently ran a "Tongue in Chic" column about the most frequently-asked questions about homeschooling. The author, Tony Silva, was having some fun with the questions before he gave the real answers:

Q: Aren't you concerned about "Socialization?"

A: Only when the neighborhood schools let out.

A: Yes! With 4-H, Scouting, the soccer team and gymnastics lessons, we almost run out of time for church services, support group socials, and school projects. Not to mention that we're sometimes too exhausted to hit the books.

A: Yes! That's why we homeschool...

A: Not really. We have the advantage of monitoring our child's peer groups. They have a variety of opportunities to interact with people of all ages and backgrounds. Their experiences are usually positive and they mature faster.[2]

As the verse from Proverbs at the beginning of the chapter reminds us, children—as well as adults—learn to pattern their behavior after the people with whom they spend the most time. We, as parents, decide with whom our children walk. If they go to public school, or even a Christian school, they will spend the majority of their time with "fools." That is not meant to be a derogatory statement about children, but it is a fact that children can be foolish. They are not the best companions and teachers for other children, especially for extended periods of time. A child who spends the majority of his waking time with other children is not walking with the wise, but with the foolish.

In an article in *The Teaching Home,* Peter and Cindy Heckroth explained why they limit the amount of peer interaction their children receive. They reported that putting children in peer groups "often causes a severe decline in the levels of attentiveness, submission, obedience, humility, kindness, and reverence that they demonstrate."[3] Because of this, they have sharply curtailed their children's contacts with peer groups.

This can sound very stifling to someone who was raised in a public school environment and spent most of his afternoons at a friend's house. But homeschool families enjoy a great deal of social interaction. The difference is the setting. The children in our family have many social contacts: they interact with peers at church, Sunday school, children's programs, and in the neighborhood. The most fulfilling for all of us, however, is time spent as a family with other families.

When we become acquainted with a family, and we trust their judgment, it is beneficial for us as a family to get together with them for an evening. The kids have a chance to socialize with children that we are comfortable with, and they can practice the skills of reaching out, playing with others, and making conversation. Because they are not directly underfoot, they can interact in their own unique styles. But they are in an environment with adults and children of different ages. They are secure in knowing that their parents are within earshot. Once we are comfortable with a family, we also take turns having their children over, so our kids get extended times to develop those friendships. This is vastly different from the "sink or swim" lessons they get by spending their entire day with a peer group.

The Negative Aspects of Peer Influence

I was once out shopping for clothing with one of my daughters. She had picked out a shirt with little flowers on it that I thought was cute, and she loved it. As we left that area of the store, two girls about her age came walking through. One of them picked up the same shirt we had just chosen, and said,

"Oh no, I wouldn't be caught dead in this!"

"Me neither, ugh!" responded the other.

Fortunately, my daughter did not hear them. I am embarrassed to admit that I almost put the shirt back! I looked at it to decide what was wrong with it, and then realized how foolish I was being. Kids make choices based on other kids' opinions, and I was delighted that my kids didn't have to use such a ridiculous standard to judge themselves. If they like flowers on their shirts, I am thankful they have the freedom to wear them.

More than that, I am thankful my children are not exposed on a daily basis to the negative, often destructive, and sometimes tragic influences that public school peers have on one another. Indeed, if the academic prob-

lems encountered in school are troubling, the social con-
duct the children learn and negative behaviors they man-
ifest should alarm us just as much. Most people know how
cruel students can be to each other—a cruelty that can
have life-long effects on a person's self-esteem if he is
exposed to it on a regular basis. Fortunately, homeschooled children can escape many of these pains of
childhood. In fact, a generation of homeschoolers "missing out" on the many negative aspects of our culture
could have a profound effect on society.

In *Home Education With Confidence*, Rick Boyer
shares how he responds to questions about socialization:

> When confronted with all the potential disaster to
> which I expose my children because I shelter them at
> home rather than turning them loose in a peer group, I
> sometimes respond with a question. I ask the concerned
> citizen to list what he considers to be the five greatest
> social problems in our country. AIDS? Violence? Teen
> pregnancy? Drugs? Divorce? Gangs? Illiteracy? There are
> quite a few to choose from. Once the list of five has been
> selected, I then ask my companion how many of those
> five he can trace to the root cause of children spending
> too much time at home?[4]

In fact, the kind of socialization many people are
concerned that homeschooled children aren't getting is
exactly the kind of socialization homeschooling parents
want to avoid. The current system of molding young lives
into the images of their peers, letting the peers set the values, and allowing other children to be the most influential aspect of a child's life, is not at all what many parents
want for their children.

It only takes a few moments to look at our society
and see some of the negative consequences of peer
dependency. Gangs, drugs, violence, and teenage promis-

cuity are all heavily attributable to the fact that children allow their decisions to be formed by the children around them. If kids spend most of their waking hours with their peers, then the consequences are clear. Our opinions and values are shaped by those that we spend the most time with. Added to this peer pressure is the media's tolerance—indeed, glorification of—much of this behavior. The resulting influence can be overwhelming, even to a child raised with traditional values.

Self-Esteem and How to Lose It

An experience I had in second grade is a classic example of peer dependency. I was a painfully shy child, unable to respond in any situation where the attention was on me and other people were watching. One day my mother fixed my hair—and put the barrette in lower than I was used to wearing it. From my adult perspective now, it was probably only one-half to one inch lower, and most likely not noticeable to anyone. But I was mortified.

I was a fairly compliant child, so, not wanting to hurt my mother's feelings, I left the barrette in. We had an assembly that day, and the girls behind me were giggling. I was so sure that they were laughing at where my hair clip was that I didn't hear one word of the assembly. There is nothing in the world to indicate that wearing a barrette in one's hair at the "wrong" spot makes one an idiot, but common sense does not come into play in peer relationships. The simple fact that no one else had done it made it unacceptable in my own eyes.

This rather insignificant incident not only shaped my opinion of hair styles, but it contributed to my already shy personality. Unhappily, the people with whom children spend their time significantly shape their sense of self-worth. This is another area in which too much time spent with peers, who are much more concerned about their own popularity than their friends' self-esteem, can be damaging.

Child psychologist Sueann Ambron, in her textbook *Child Development*, states:

> The child's self-esteem is, essentially, his self-judgment of his own abilities, influence, and popularity. To a certain extent, it is a mirror image of the judgment of others. His degree of self-esteem will affect his behavior by limiting or extending the range of things he will attempt, whether in academic tasks, sports, or friendships. Low self-esteem tends to make the child less original and more imitative, whereas high self-esteem brings out initiative and independent judgment.[5]

According to her, and other psychologists as well, how children behave has a great deal to do with their self-esteem. While many factors affect a child's self-esteem, and many events and attitudes contribute to it, self-esteem is formed largely by how others treat us. If a child is reaffirmed and built up, he can develop into a confident, wise adult. If he is unsure of himself, and is frequently teased or ridiculed, his self-esteem may never develop properly. It stands to reason, then, that too much exposure to peers can seriously inhibit a child's self-image.

Similarly, just as my barrette incident as a child influenced the way I did my hair, children's attitudes toward physical appearance can affect their self-worth.

Psychologist James Dobson, a recognized authority on children and issues relating to the family, says:

> The current epidemic of self-doubt is primarily the result of a totally unjust and unnecessary system of evaluating human worth now prevalent in our society. Not everyone is seen as worthy; not everyone is accepted.

79

Instead, we reserve our praise and admiration for a select few who have been blessed from birth with the characteristics we value most highly. It is a vicious system, and we, as parents, must counterbalance its impact.

It seems that human worth in our society is carefully reserved for those who meet certain rigid specifications. The beautiful people are born with it; those who are highly intelligent are likely to find approval; superstar athletes are usually respected. But no one is considered valuable just because he is! Social acceptability is awarded rather carefully, making certain to exclude those who are unqualified.[6]

School children accept this system of approval before they realize what they are doing. It then becomes so much a part of the social structure that they cannot break away from it. Therefore, the first few years of elementary school can determine the future for many children.

The importance of the early school years in establishing a child's own image of how he can perform cannot be overemphasized. The public school system offers very little positive influence at this stage. Similarly, though possibly not quite as much, a private school environment can also negatively affect a child's faith in his own abilities. Although classes may be smaller, and teachers may have more time to foster kinder attitudes among the students, the child still spends the majority of his time with other students and thus may be greatly affected by their evaluation of him.

Dobson maintains that the majority of children will emerge from the school system with the conviction that they are unintelligent and stupid. He says that many students fall into one of the following categories: the slow learner, the semi-literate child, the underachiever, the culturally deprived child, or the late bloomer. Each of these students concludes that he is not bright enough to succeed, but each of them can learn if the right tools are used and a sense of acceptance is communicated. As he says, "It is appalling to recognize that the children in these five categories actually outnumber those students who feel successful in school!"[7] We see that spending the school years with kids who are equally immature can have far-reaching results.

A Better Method

Anne Shirley, the impetuous orphan in the classic *Anne of Green Gables*, had a head of gorgeous red hair. Anne had decided that her hair was the ugliest burden she could carry, and she began her first day at a new school with a defensive attitude.

> Gilbert Blythe wasn't used to putting himself out to make a girl look at him and meeting with failure. She should look at him, the red-haired Shirley girl with the little pointed chin and the big eyes that weren't like the eyes of any other girl in Avonlea school.
>
> Gilbert reached across the aisle, picked up the end of Anne's long read braid, held it out at arm's length and said in a piercing whisper,
>
> "Carrots! Carrots!!"
>
> Then Anne looked at him with a vengeance!
>
> She did more than look. She sprang to her feet, her bright fancies fallen into cureless ruin. She flashed one indignant glance at Gilbert from eyes whose angry sparkle was swiftly quenched in equally angry tears.
>
> "You mean, hateful boy!" she exclaimed passionately. "How dare you!!"
>
> And then!!
>
> Thwack! Anne had brought her slate down on Gilbert's head and cracked it—slate, not head—clear across.[8]

Unfortunately, most girls aren't apt to fight back when they are ridiculed, and instead withdraw. As the story develops, Anne's hair color is not really the issue; Gilbert just wants her attention. Even so, as an adult, she saw her hair as ugly and undesirable. Though she ends up marrying Gilbert in the next book, she can't get to the point where she likes the color of her hair.

If children are continually told they are weird, or different, or slow, they will believe it. Even if they have other experiences as they grow older, the old tapes about how worthless they are will hold a dominant place in their minds. Of course, the opposite is true also. Students who are told they are beautiful, smart, or talented, will carry that confidence with them for a long time. Many will even develop those qualities because they believe they have them. It is wonderful to see a child have his confidence boosted and then excel in that area. Did his skills suddenly improve, or his knowledge increase? Most likely, the simple confidence that he could do it made the difference.

That doesn't mean that homeschoolers are constantly telling their children how wonderful they are. That, of course, would be ridiculous. But homeschooled children know that when Mom tells them that number eight is wrong on their math paper, they are not thereby worthless. They take all knowledge, correction, and teaching on the basis that they are loved, cared for, and valuable. Even through the difficult times, and the subjects they don't understand, they are almost never led to believe they are stupid or can't get it. They always have that underlying foundation of knowing they are accepted and important, and that they have a purpose in life. What better way to mold a child into a confident, intelligent, responsible adult?

As a child I had difficulty with math. I struggled over it, cried over it, and tried to hide the fact that it was difficult. Though I didn't mind seeking help at home, I rarely wanted to admit in the classroom that I didn't get it. I lived in fear that we would play "around the world"—a math facts game—and I would mess up and be "out." After one bad year of math, I was convinced I was not very bright, and didn't do well in it for years. But in junior high, I got a high grade in a math class, and decided, as a consequence, that maybe I wasn't so stupid. Interestingly enough, I began doing better. I ended up taking trigonometry. But I could have let myself consistently underachieve in math if I had not done well once, and then been encouraged at home.

Similarly, my oldest daughter struggles with math. She cries over it at times. But she is not terrified of doing it. She doesn't think that she is stupid, or that she will never be good in math. Because I can work with her on the areas in which she is weak, and coach her through the tough days, math is simply a subject she has to work on, and her struggle does not become an all-out assault on her self-esteem.

Accentuate the Positive

Homeschooled children can learn patterns of interaction that include respect and manners, as opposed to the typical interaction among public school peers. Rarely do adults call each other names, ignore each other, or ridicule one another because of one small mistake. At home, children can learn healthy—rather than unhealthy—ways of dealing with others. In some areas, peer groups have become isolated from all other society, forming a tight-knit group that establishes its own rules and communication. Kids who are involved in these groups have very little interest in the teaching and input of their parents, and are less likely to follow their rules and respect their values. Though this sounds like a gang, it is more of a clique. Such peer dependence for status and behavior is not in the best interest of the family or the child.

Many people claim that a child who spends too much time with adults will be "weird," or a social misfit. In extreme circumstances, this could be true. But very few homeschool families live in a child-deprived culture. Child-raising is probably the only scenario where people would actually believe that providing a superior role model is harmful.

For example, suppose you wanted your grandchild to learn to play the piano. You have a choice between two teachers: the first, a superb classical pianist, who has been playing her whole life and loves the child; the second, a teenager who is just learning to play. You are not likely to choose the teenager, saying, "She just shouldn't be exposed to someone who has this mastered. We need to let her learn from someone who is closer to her own age." This would be absurd. You want the best possible teacher—the person that will demonstrate the best skill. So it is equally as pointless to expect children to grow up into adults, yet give them only other children as models for their behavior.

In fact, the family is the best place for socialization available. Children can learn the social skills, manners, and courtesies they need in the setting of their own homes. Then they can practice those skills in public. Family interactions can provide the necessary ingredients for social development, because the family provides "love, security, discipline, interdependence and responsibility. Friends outside the family are important, but they don't have to be present every day for the formation of socially well-developed individuals."[9]

Studies Show Home Socialization Works

Experts and parents alike are beginning to question whether peer socialization—where children learn from other children, and derive their values from the youth culture rather than from their church or their parents— is really the best form of socialization, especially considering the number of troubled, peer-dependent, amoral youth today, and the problems they create for society. However, all the talk about how superior homeschoolers' "family-style" socialization is when compared to modern society's peer socialization is meaningless if homeschooled children are coming into the world as social outcasts, unable to handle people or to communicate effectively with others. (They are not, as anyone that knows a homeschooler will tell you!)

Happily, the research on the socialization of homeschoolers affirms what their parents know and believe about the value of socialization monitored and directed by parents rather than peers.

Brian Ray's pamphlet *Marching to the Beat of Their Own Drum* details many studies that have been done to measure the socialization of homeschooled students. In one of these studies, Dr. Kathie Johnson researched ways homeschoolers sought to meet the needs of socialization. She found that parents ". . . indicated numerous ways in which they have established stable, close, respectful relationships with their students and have provided controlled access to others as well."[10]

The pamphlet describes many other studies that

have been made on the socialization of homeschooled students, summarized as follows:

Dr. Wesley Taylor focused on self-concept as an important aspect of the psychological development of children and studied 224 homeschooled students in grades four through twelve to see whether a positive self-concept is related to positive socialization. He discovered that the self-concept of home school students was significantly higher than that of public school students on each one of the scales he measured.

Dr. Mona Delahooke compared students in private and home school situations, and found that private-schooled children were more concerned with the opinions of their peers than the homeschooled groups, and that home-educated children considered their parents the primary authority more often than the private school children.

Dr. Larry Shyers compared the social adjustment of home and traditionally schooled children, interviewing only children that had been educated exclusively either at home or in the public school, i.e., he didn't use anyone that had been in both situations. He found some similarities in the two groups: both scored above the national average on self-concept tests, and both received scores that indicated they choose passive responses over aggressive responses to social situations. He also discovered important differences. The children were videotaped in free play and group interaction, and were observed by trained people that did not know which group was which. The traditionally schooled students received significantly higher problem behavior scores than did their home schooled age-mates. The students from traditional schools were louder, more aggressive, and more competitive.

Another researcher studied to what degree home

schooled children were exposed to or provided with situations that encouraged the development of leadership skills. Focusing on kids aged ten to twenty-one, Dr. Linda Montgomery found that homeschooled students are involved in youth groups, church activities, sports, and similar activities. She concluded that homeschooling may nurture leadership as well or better than do conventional schools.

Dr. J. Gary Knowles was the first to focus on home educated adults. Collecting data from a group that was home schooled an average of six years before the age of seventeen, he found that their occupations were entrepreneurial and professional, and that they were fiercely independent and very committed to their families. In addition, they were glad they had been home educated, and would recommend it to others.[11]

Rick Boyer sums it up perfectly:

> This goes to show that a person's ability to get along with others doesn't depend on having enough time with Kids Their Own Age. A look at the lives of those who grew up free of age segregation is a better indicator than the dire predictions of conventional wisdom and pop psychology.[12]

It appears, then, that the socialization of kids who are homeschooled is more than adequate; in fact, in terms of positive socialization, it is probably superior to that of most other children. Parents who homeschool provide their children with a variety of activities and experiences that increase their social skills. Unlike public school children, who are thrown in with their peers for the better part of each day, homeschooled children develop socialization skills within positive, carefully chosen groups that have a common purpose.

What About Real Life?

Another aspect of the socialization issue is the question of "real life." "Kids need to find out what real life is," skeptics argue. "How can they function in the real world if they have never experienced it?"

The accusation that homeschooling is not "real life" just doesn't hold up when examined carefully. In fact, it is public school life that doesn't mimic the "real world" very closely. Chris Klicka, in his book *The Right Choice: The Incredible Failure of Public Education and the Rising Hope of Homeschooling,* characterizes a classroom as a place where children are trapped with kids their own age with little interaction with adults. They are given very little responsibility, he states, with too much provided for them. The actions by the students rarely have consequences, and they are passed to the next grade regardless of their behavior. None of this, he says, prepares students for the home or work place—the "real world" they will be entering as adults.[13]

One aspect of public schools that is usually not a part of homeschools is competition, and there are those that argue that homeschooled kids need to experience the competitive, aggressive nature of other children in order to survive the rigors of public life. But this may not be true either. As Rick Boyer reminds us:

> One of the most common arguments for subjecting children to the peer pressure of school is that they are getting ready to enter a world full of pressure and need to "get used to it." That's wrong. On the contrary, children in schools are already in the world of pressure, and most of them will face much less pressure, at least socially, as adults. When I was a school boy I moved daily in an environment where my physical safety was threatened by

bigger boys needing to prove their machismo, where verbalizing a wrong answer could bring howls of scornful laughter and where the rudest contempt was regularly heaped on those who did poorly on tests, or couldn't run as fast as others on the playground. Rudeness, bullying, exclusion, mockery and cliques were the order of the day. To say that is good for child's soul or mind is tantamount to saying that eating garbage will make his body healthy.

It's also silly to say that it prepares a child for the "real world." I live in the real world, and people don't act that way here. Anyone who did would stand a good chance of losing friends, his job, and any degree of respect in the eyes of the community. Yet in school society such obnoxiousness is business as usual.[14]

Children will have to enter the public life as they get older. But there is nothing to indicate that throwing them in at five years of age, unprepared and open to any teaching, is more effective than introducing them to difficult situations one at a time. They will have a much easier time of it if they enter the public arena at an older age, with confidence and security under their belts.

Yes, the world is rough. But it makes more sense to build up children in their faith, nurture them, and teach them, while they are young, and then, as their strength grows, slowly introduce them to competitive and difficult situations. Only in this way will they grow into competent, confident, adults. Rick Boyer states this well:

I've heard a number of people espouse the idea that the way to teach children to stand alone is to throw them out of the nest and let them fight it out in the coliseum from early on. May I say I am appalled at just how stupid that idea is. Any animal on the upper end of the food chain has the sense to protect and train its young through intense personal contact until they can do the things which the adults of the species do. Imagine a lioness deserting her half-grown cubs to hunt zebras on their own. They'd get their teeth kicked out. But we do that very thing when we send our young children to school. We force them to face social pressures that in some ways are greater than those of the adult world. Do we really expect them to stand alone in the company of who-knows-whose kids? At five years of age?[15]

The socialization issue will probably be raised as long as there are people that are skeptical about homeschooling, and it will be resolved as soon as those skeptics see the visible fruit of homeschooling: bright, articulate, well-mannered, poised, homeschooled young people making their way in the world. When a critic looks at the research regarding negative socialization and observes the success with which homeschoolers are socialized, he will see that homeschoolers are, in all likelihood, the best prepared for what this world has to offer to adults.

Chapter Five

······················

Is it Legal? Then and Now

THEN HE SAID TO THEM, "GIVE TO CAESAR WHAT
IS CAESAR'S, AND TO GOD WHAT IS GOD'S."
—MATTHEW 22:21

Dorothy Ferguson was fearful of the legal consequences when her daughter Mary Lou Anderson began home-schooling. Her fears were compounded when Mary Lou reported that a social worker had come to the house. Mary Lou explained to the worker that what she was doing was legal, but Dorothy was afraid the neighbors would complain and the worker would return.

While this type of confrontation was common when the homeschooling movement began, it happens less frequently today, because homeschooling is now legal in all states.

A Little History

There was a time in our country when there were no laws against homeschooling. In fact, homeschooling was his-torically the most common form of education in the United States until a little over one hundred years ago, when it declined as an educational option to the point where it had become, by the mid 1900's, nearly extinct. By then, laws had been passed mandating compulsory (public) schooling. These laws were originally created to eliminate the abuses of child labor and to insure the education of immigrant children—but they were later used by government officials, when the homeschooling movement began to grow, to attempt to prevent parents from homeschooling. These laws were challenged in states all around the country.

As Chris Klicka tells us,

> The legal road to home schooling . . . has not been easy, since most states did not formally recognize the right of parents to home school their own children. In 1980, only three states in the entire country, Utah, Ohio, and Nevada, officially recognized the right to home school in their state statutes. In most states, it was "open season" on families teaching their children at home, and they were often prosecuted under criminal truancy laws and educational neglect charges.
>
> . . .[However,] the national trend [is] to limit state controls over private education in favor of expanding parental liberty. Since 1982, thirty-two states have changed their compulsory attendance laws, and four State Boards of Education have amended their regulations to specifically allow for home schooling, with certain minimal requirements.[1]

State Requirements

So what are these minimal requirements? Most of them deal with reporting, testing, and attendance. Having guidelines is a positive thing, because in the case of disputes, each case must be decided according to the mandates of the law and not according to the opinion of a judge, who may be prejudiced against homeschooling.

Several states require a letter of intent that verifies that instruction will be provided in a core group of subjects. This letter usually states which children will be taught at home and what subjects will be covered. This puts the families on an honor system that leaves it up to them to follow through. Since homeschool families want a good education for their children, they obviously have no interest in cheating the system. This situation is ideal, and you can rest assured that if your family lives in a state with this requirement, they will probably not encounter any legal difficulties as a result of their homeschooling.

Some states also require parents to test their children at certain intervals, but do not require them to submit the scores to school authorities. The parents thus receive feedback about their children's progress, but the public schools are not given any control over the outcome. Most homeschool parents test their children anyway, because of the desire to make sure their children have acquired the skills appropriate for their grade levels.

The laws of other states require the homeschool parent to administer standardized tests or be under the evaluation of an approved teacher. These states require students to score at a certain level or lose their right to homeschool, which is one reason homeschoolers object to submitting test scores. Another reason is that most families believe that it is not the government's right to evaluate their children, and they seek to have those laws repealed. Low test scores are rarely a problem with homeschooled kids because, as I have noted previously, most homeschoolers score significantly higher on achievement tests than do public school students. Still, the threat of interference is a serious concern for parents who have just begun to homeschool and haven't had time to raise test scores, or whose children have a certain disability or difficulty that makes a high score unlikely.

Another requirement in some states is that of teacher certification. This is a very touchy subject, because research has shown that teacher certification, or training, or even whether the teacher has a college degree has little or no bearing on the student's achievement.[2] But some states insist that a certified teacher must have some role in the homeschool. Although many of these laws change every year, and the emphasis on teacher training is decreasing, this issue still pops up frequently. During the voting process of Goals 2000, for instance, an effort was made to require all teachers—nationwide—in private and home schools to be certified. This was a terrible threat to private religious schools—which often employ teachers that are not certified—as well as to homeschool families, and the public outcry resulted in the defeat of that requirement.

As you can see, although homeschooling is legal in all fifty states, there are many variations in the states' requirements, and some states have more requirements than others. Wise parents therefore prepare ahead of time: they learn their state's requirements and make sure everything is in order before they begin. Families that go into homeschooling with too little thought or preparation may encounter many more stumbling blocks than those that have done their homework. Ideally, a family should make the decision to homeschool several months before the beginning of the upcoming school year. This is especially true if they live in states that require notification to the school district before beginning. If parents are schooling older children, or are pulling them out of a public school system, preparation still works in their favor.

Another reason parents need to be aware of their

state's requirements is that the laws can change. The changes are made for various reasons, but typically they are made to eliminate the abuses of authority to which school officials can be prone. For example, at one time Colorado had a law requiring parents to test their children with the same test "used by the local school district of residence," but now they may use any national standardized achievement test they choose. The new law also deleted the requirements for age equivalent testing.[3]

Information about the current legal status of homeschooling in your state can be found through local support groups or by contacting the Home School Legal Defense Association, a national organization established for the purpose of assisting homeschoolers in their efforts to homeschool legally. It's the best kind of insurance a homeschool family can buy.

The Home School Legal Defense Association

Several years ago my husband and I were house-hunting, and we toured a home that obviously had small children living in it. I asked the realtor why these people were selling a house that seemed to be so well suited for them. Sadly the realtor shook his head.

"The baby that lives in this house was born premature, and the parents didn't have any insurance. After over a month in intensive care at Children's Hospital, the bills are astronomical. They think that by selling they can put the equity towards the debt."

"How much do they owe?"

"Over $80,000."

I gasped. "Then the house equity will hardly make a dent in it!"

"You're right. Like a drop in a very large bucket."

* * * *

I felt so badly for those people that wanted to stay in their house, but didn't know what else to do to pay off those huge bills. Living without insurance can come with a very large price tag.

In today's world, very few people would consider going through life without car insurance, house insurance, health insurance, and life insurance. Does that mean we are all convinced that we will be in a car accident, have our house burn down, and be diagnosed with a deadly disease? No, in fact, we all hope that we won't ever have a need for such insurance. But we know there is a chance we will, so we pay the money "just in case."

The same reasoning causes homeschoolers to join the Home School Legal Defense Association, an organization founded by homeschooling attorneys. They state in their membership application leaflet: "The purpose of the Home School Legal Defense Association is to bring together a large number of home schooling families so that each can have a low-cost method of obtaining quality legal defense. We give families the freedom to home school without the fear of facing legal threats alone."

For many homeschoolers, their HSLDA membership is an insurance policy. For $100 a year, they know they have legal representation as close as a phone call away. If a member homeschooler has any negative encounter with a public official, he simply calls HSLDA. HSLDA frequently settles the matter with a letter or a phone call, referring to the homeschool laws in that state and discussing the matter with the official. Their staff of highly knowledgeable lawyers is almost always better informed than the school officials. In cases where more action is necessary, HSLDA does all the legal research and represents the family in court.

HSLDA also publishes *Home Schooling in the United States: A Legal Analysis,* a book that summarizes the laws in all fifty states. It contains a one-page summary for each state, quoting the laws on the books and listing all the requirements for that state. It is a wonderful tool for people that move from state to state. In addition, HSLDA publishes *The Home School Court Report,* a magazine that provides members with updates of the legal situation of homeschooling across the country. The magazine *The Teaching Home* also features a column written by HSLDA staff members that summarizes any changes in the homeschooling laws in all states.

Thanks to HSLDA, homeschoolers can remain abreast of the law and protect themselves as well. As the organization likes to say in its publications, "Don't stay home without it!"

It is thanks to the hard work of pioneer homeschooling families and organizations such as HSLDA that homeschooling is protected and preserved almost everywhere in the United States.

Chapter Six

. . . .

Ways and Means:
Curriculum Materials,
Teaching Approaches, and
Support Groups

One crystal clear Colorado day, my sister Beth and a friend decided to try their luck at rollerblading. They headed for the mountains, stopping first at a rental shop where they were outfitted with all the garb: kneepads, wrist pads, and most importantly, the blades.

They decided the best place to begin was in Boulder Canyon, along a beautiful stretch of pathway that winds along a wooded valley—in the trees away from the highway, with no cars to interfere with the bikers and joggers.

Eagerly they strapped on their skates and pushed off onto the blacktop. Since neither one had gone rollerblading before, they began with the uphill section and planned to return downhill.

After gliding a few feet, my sister yelled up to her friend, "Hey, Colleen! Have you figured out how to stop yet?"

"Yeah, I think so. You head for the grass like this" — she veered to the right — "and kind of jog-trip-cartwheel until you stop. See?" Colleen demonstrated the fine technique while my sister watched skeptically.

"O.K." she said. "I guess I'll try it when I need it."

Reaching the top of the hill, they were ready for the downhill section. From the top, they realized going up wasn't the same as going down, and that the bikes headed downhill were flying.

Undaunted, they began the trip down. My sister gathered speed, enjoying the breeze in her hair Up ahead, the path curved slightly, and she practiced leaning to the left to make the skates turn. Suddenly the curve wasn't ahead, but upon her, and her leaning wasn't turning her in the same angle as the road. Her panic mounted as the pavement ending approached and one more fact dawned on her: there was no grass here to make the stop.

Glancing ahead, she saw Colleen trying to stop, but cartwheeling headlong into the pavement instead. Losing what little concentration she had left, her balance faltered, and she collided with the blacktop. She felt the rocks scraping the flesh off her thigh as she skidded to a stop in a heap. Fighting back the tears, she examined the damage, realizing she couldn't even skate back to where they had left the car. Although Colleen's fall was more spectacular, she wasn't hurt too badly.

It was six years before my sister got on rollerblades again. And when she did, she was very nervous. Although we all tease her about the incident, the fact is she could have been seriously injured. She realizes now that undertaking a new sport requires learning all the moves, especially how to stop.

* * * * *

Though homeschooling is not physically as dangerous as rollerblading, it does require preparation. The mother who jumps into it on a whim with no thought about the process involved will feel a little like my sister: heading way too fast in a direction that is unfamiliar. Proper preparation will enable the new homeschooler to avoid such a catastrophe.

What Material Is Available for Homeschoolers?

One of the questions I receive frequently from non-homeschoolers is "How do you know what to teach? Do you get textbooks and stuff?" Grandparents, especially, have this concern.

When Linda, Polly Gilpin's homeschooling daughter, tried to explain to her mother the great amount of home-schooling material available, Polly was confused: "Linda came home [from a homeschool convention] very excited and wanted to show me all her 'goodies' on curriculum. (Curriculum? What is that ? . . .)"[1]

Many people don't realize that today there is a wealth of material available for teaching children. (I think some people truly believe that homeschoolers use slates and ABC cards and make up the rest on their own.) It is true that as recently as ten years ago, there were very few materials available, and many of them were geared to classroom use. Pioneer homeschoolers adapted curricula, made up their own, or used the encyclopedia and old textbooks. Today, however, the sheer volume of options to homeschoolers is enough to overwhelm anyone just getting into it. Many of the publishers of Christian school materials offer a whole line of products to homeschoolers. Some companies are designed with homeschoolers in mind, and sell materials specifically designed for a homeschool setting. Curriculum fairs and curriculum guides are packed to overflowing with information and teaching materials, and there are few things homeschool moms enjoy more than poring through the catalogues and ordering next year's material. In fact, I get calls from people as early as January asking me what I am going to use next year and how I liked such-and-such curriculum.

I have a friend who has four small children and one on the way, and she had plans one year to attend a curriculum fair. A week before the fair, she got the chicken pox. Anyone that is familiar with the chicken pox knows that adults that get the disease become very ill. In the beginning days of her sickness, I called her to ask how she was doing. She told me that she wasn't feeling too badly, but was upset because she was going to miss the curriculum fair.

"There will be other chances to get your curriculum," I consoled her.

"I know, but I wanted to do it now. I am really disappointed."

This is a typical response from homeschool moms—don't stand in the way of them and their curriculum!

Although attending a curriculum fair is the best way to become acquainted with homeschool materials, there are several books that review curriculum, and also numerous catalog suppliers of homeschool materials—a number of which I have listed in the appendix. An examination of these resources should remove any doubts you may have about the availability of high-quality textbooks and teaching resources. The books and catalogs will provide you with invaluable information about homeschool materials and allow you to locate specific items of interest. A grandparent who is familiar with what is available for her homeschooling grandchildren will be well-equipped to support them in their studies.

Information on a wide variety of teaching approaches is also readily available. In the following pages I will summarize the most popular of those approaches. In the appendix, I have listed some of the books that homeschoolers have found most useful in gaining an understanding of the various teaching approaches.

Teaching Approaches

A new homeschool mom begins by taking a good, hard look at her child. She determines how he learns, what he likes, what his strengths and weaknesses are, and how mature he is. With this information, and information about herself and her family, she then chooses the teaching approaches that are best for her needs. There are many approaches available to homeschooling parents, but most homeschoolers begin with the traditional (textbook) method.

THE TEXTBOOK METHOD

This is probably the most common approach to homeschooling, especially for those who are new to the field. Because it is most similar to public schools in its work format, and because it is very easy for teachers to use, it is frequently the best place to begin when teaching children at home.

The textbook method is what most people are visualizing when we say the word "school." It uses textbooks and workbooks developed by Christian publishers for the various grade levels. Each publisher's books have unique characteristics that set them apart from the books of other publishers, but they all cover similar topics at any given grade level.

The main difference between Christian homeschool texts and public school texts is the Christian context, which influences every aspect of many textbooks. For instance, instead of plain math problems, students may be asked to calculate a tithe on an allowance of $5.00, or figure out the total number of missionaries in three different countries combined.

Although the Christian influence can be seen in textbooks on every subject, it is most prominent in the history books. Many secular history books have carefully weeded out most references to Christianity. Christian textbooks discuss the character and lifestyle of prominent historical figures that were Christians. Since many of our founding fathers quoted Scripture in their writings and speeches, learning about their Christian character gives a much different flavor to the children's study of history.

For example, the following passage from a second grade Christian history textbook explains the meetings the founding fathers held when they drafted the Constitution, and Benjamin Franklin's contributions to those meetings:

> The new set of laws would be called the Constitution of the United States.
> By now, Benjamin Franklin was 81 years old, but his age did not stop him from attending the many meetings. He was the oldest man there.
> At first there were many arguments in these meetings. Ben became a peacemaker. Once when the men were arguing, he stood up and suggested that each meeting be opened with prayer. They became quiet as he spoke:
> "I have lived a long time, and the longer I live the

more convincing proofs I see of this truth: that God governs in the affairs of men. And if a sparrow cannot fall to the ground without his notice, is it probable that an empire [great country] can rise without his aid?"

Ben sat back down. There was no prayer, but the men calmed down. They continued their meetings with fewer arguments.[2]

This excerpt is typical of material found in many textbooks used in the traditional approach. Many homeschoolers start out with this approach and, as they get more comfortable, experiment with other methods. In fact, many new homeschoolers will just order the complete line of curriculum from one company to be sure they are getting complete coverage in every subject. Then, as they develop their own teaching styles and become familiar with the learning styles of their students, they branch out.

THE CLASSICAL APPROACH

Brenda Kelly summarizes the classical method of education in this way:

> The idea behind the classical approach is to teach the tools of learning so that they may be used in the study of any subject. These tools (called the Trivium) are: Grammar (the mastery of facts), Dialectic (the study of logic), and Rhetoric (the expressive or creative use of language.)[3]

The magazine *Practical Homeschooling* carries a column by Doug Wilson about classical education. This is his explanation of the classical approach:

> The purpose of following this pattern is not to teach the student everything there is to know, but

rather to establish in the student a habit of mind which instinctively knows how to learn new material when the formal schooling process is only a faint memory. The student is not so much taught what to think, he is shown how to think.[4]

He goes on to explain that classical instruction also teaches students the rigors of logical analysis. This teaches students to sort out fact from fiction, and to be able to determine how worthwhile an argument is. This aspect of classical education is not as predominant in the other approaches.

Although Mr. Wilson says that the classical approach isn't for every student, he says that some of our children must receive such an education, for the good of us all. Classical learning is ideally suited for the training of cultural leaders.

THE UNIT STUDY APPROACH

One of the most popular alternatives to a traditional education is the unit study approach, which may be described as follows:

> The concept of unit studies is that all knowledge is interrelated and is learned more easily and remembered longer if presented in this related way. A unit study is taking a theme or topic (a unit of study) and delving into it deeply over a period of time, integrating language arts, social studies, science, history, math and fine arts as they apply.[5]

Unit studies address many subjects within one unit, reducing the fragmentation that can occur when subjects are studied separately. Jessica Hulcy, a woman who writes a column on unit studies in *Practical Homeschooling*,

106

describes her own education in unit studies:

> As a young girl my father took our family on month long trips across the United States. Since we traveled with 400 National Geographics in the back seat of our station wagon, these trips were both fun and educational.
>
> Somehow, on these treks across America, my father showed me the "connectedness" of the world. Monticello wasn't just about the man Thomas Jefferson. Monticello embodied architecture in the buildings, botany in the gardens, history in Jefferson's political achievements, and a world view of how men should be treated in the written words of the Declaration of Independence.
>
> I wanted to impart this same "connectedness" of the world to my children when I began homeschooling, so I chose unit studies as the "connector" of subjects. Under unit themes, subjects fit together, giving them meaning. If "trust" is the theme, our focus is on sheep trusting their shepherd for their every need. Children memorize the 23rd Psalm (Bible), examine similes, metaphors and analogies in the 23rd Psalm (English), study the habits and traits of sheep (science), research the actual responsibilities and duties of a shepherd (history), read the Newbery Award winner . . . And Now Miguel, which is the story of a shepherd boy's life (literature), and lastly, card, spin, and weave sheep's wool (art). Units provide a multitude of topics connected by a theme.[6]

People that use a unit study approach have a variety of reasons for doing so. Many people get tired of the workbook routine in all subjects, and want to delve deeper into some topics. Others like the freedom and creativity involved in planning lessons. The author of the above column says that she likes the relationships it builds in her family, as they all work together on a project. It seems that more and more homeschooling families are turning to unit studies for variety in their approach to teaching.

Especially as students get into the upper grades, unit studies will continue to offer a great alternative to traditional styles of schooling.

THE PRINCIPLE APPROACH

The principle approach is founded on the idea that our nation is a unique and vital link in the chain of the Christian faith, and one of its goals is to educate young Christians to live victorious lives today and become the leaders of tomorrow. Children learn to evaluate current issues from a Christian perspective, and they also approach many of their subjects, particularly history, economics, law, and literature by studying them through a rigorously Christian worldview. As one advocate describes it:

> The approach is an effort to restore to American Christians three vital concepts: the knowledge of our Christian history; an understanding of our role in the spread of Christianity; and the ability to live according to the biblical principles upon which our country was founded. The Principle Approach is a way of living life, not just a way of educating children.[7]

The Nehemiah Institute has developed a test that measures how biblical or non-biblical a student's worldview is, called the PEERS test. It measures the student's response to one hundred statements concerning politics, economics, etc. The results of this test have been somewhat predictable, in that Christian day and homeschool students scored significantly higher than public school students. But last year the institute's director was surprised to find that students taught with the principle approach scored far higher than all the rest. In fact, "the gap in scores between students taught through the principle approach and those of other Christian pupils is greater than the gap between the other Christian students and pupils in public schools."[8]

LIVING BOOKS AND
THE CHARLOTTE MASON APPROACH

Charlotte Mason was a British educator at the turn of the century who was instrumental in the establishment of parent-controlled schools, and whose educational philosophy influenced many families in the education of their children. Education was, for her, "an atmosphere, a discipline, a life." She believed that it was the parents' responsibility to provide a home atmosphere that encouraged the formation of lifelong habits, academic and physical, as well as spiritual. For the early school years she believed in short lessons and ample time for outside activity. Oral, and then written, narration replaced tests, homework, and grades as a means for the teacher to measure student comprehension and progress. She was not very enthusiastic about textbooks, and thought that most of them were dry and deadening to the imagination of the child. Instead, she encouraged the use of what she called "living books," living in the sense that they are "written by a single author who shares his favorite subject with us and we pick up his enthusiasm."[9]

The goal of the parent-teachers was to inculcate in the children good habits and a love of learning for its own sake, providing them with the discipline and the desire to allow them to assume responsibility for their own education. Charlotte Mason thought we ought to educate children for life, and in such a way that throughout their lives they pursue the never-ending adventure of learning.

How Fast? Some Different Approaches

We have seen that one advantage of homeshooling over other teaching situations is that the teaching can be tailored to fit the individual child. Some of that tailoring focuses on how fast the student will progress through his studies and some focuses on when to begin schooling in general.

ACCELERATED EDUCATION

Accelerated education is just what it sounds like: moving students through their education at a faster rate than the average. Proponents of accelerated education, like Mrs. Joyce Swann, say that the goal is to educate children without taking meandering forays that would bring nothing to the learning process and could act as an impediment to learning.[10]

In other words, teachers taking this approach develop a tight program to accomplish the basics, and keep moving at a vigorous pace. Most people who are committed to accelerated education keep very strict school hours and do school year-round. Mrs. Swann reports that her children maintain a schedule of three hours a day, five days a week, twelve months a year. With this regimen, kids usually graduate from high school several years before the norm, and then move into correspondence courses or some type of college level course work.

DELAYED LEARNING VERSUS EARLY ACADEMICS

Two approaches to early education are directly opposite: delayed learning and early academics. These are not really approaches, but two philosophies about when children should begin formal schooling.

Advocates of delayed learning believe that forcing a

child into academic subjects at an early age can actually be harmful to the child's learning. They therefore believe in delaying formal education in the subjects of reading, writing, and arithmetic and putting the emphasis in early childhood on practical experience instead. "Key elements of this approach include readiness, parental involvement, informality, and the balanced development of 'head, heart, hand, and health.'"[11]

This approach is dealt with at length in the book *Better Late Than Early,* by Raymond and Dorothy Moore, in which the authors use much scientific research and data to explain their theory that many children are not ideally ready for a school setting until they are between eight and ten years old. They state:

> Early childhood education must take into account the development of the child's brain, vision, hearing, perception, emotions, sociability, family and school relationships and physical growth. For each of these factors, there appears to be a level of maturity at which most children can, without serious risk, leave normal homes and begin typical school tasks . . . On the basis of a comprehensive review of many research findings outlined in the following chapters, we believe that the IML [child's maturity level] is seldom, if ever, achieved earlier than ages 8–10.[12]

Parents that adopt this philosophy usually delay their children's formal education until the age of eight or ten.

Proponents of early academics, on the other hand, stress developing each child spiritually, morally, and academically while the brain is still young. The approach involves structured training periods that are geared to the child's attention span. It does not require that parents maintain a strict classroom environment, but it does mean they will establish and enforce reasonable goals when the child is at a young age.[13]

Books advocating each of these educational philosophies are available at libraries, Christian book stores, and in book catalogues. I encourage interested grandparents to seek further information from these sources.

Can all of these methods be right? Yes, they can. Even though many of the philosophies appear to contradict each other, they all have merit. Many parents find that they have one child that thrives under one approach, and another that responds to a different style. Blending styles is quite possible, too. For example, I use the traditional method for my "three R's," but incorporate many of the unit study ideas into my history lessons. Similarly, some parents simply couldn't teach using certain approaches, while certain others suit them just fine. Every family is different, and every child is different. Instead of trying to find the "perfect" approach to homeschooling, parents explore the possibilities and decide on a method —or methods— that will work well with their family, taking into account their schedules, and their various personalities.

Many parents find that a change of approach is necessary as children get older. Some start with a traditional approach when they begin homeschooling, but move into unit studies as they get more comfortable. Still others try one approach for a year, and then try another the next. Hopefully, this summary has given you some idea about the different approaches, so that you can be familiar with what your grandchildren may be doing.

Support Groups

As well as selecting materials and teaching styles, the new homeschool mom needs to seek out a support group.

Why? For the same reasons people in any situation need contact with others that are experiencing similar challenges. Support groups offer field trips for the kids, newsletters, and moms' discussion groups. But their greatest value is as a way to meet and build friendships with women who have similar interests and concerns.

Traditional support groups are built on the concept that people who have experienced a certain stress are able to help others deal with that same stress. Although home-school support groups are not formed for the purpose of helping people deal with stress, they can offer substantial emotional and practical help to homeschoolers. Homeschool support groups of varying sizes are in every city and community. Larger cities have support groups in every neighborhood or every suburb of the city. In rural areas, the support group may be county-wide, or be comprised of homeschoolers from several counties.

When I began to homeschool, I was only vaguely acquainted with anyone else that did it. While my friends were driving their children to the public school every morning, I was taking mine for a walk. When they were picking their children up, mine were in the bedroom playing. Differences such as these can cause a mother to feel more isolated in her role as a homeschool mom. After a year or two, I knew several moms who were homeschooling. Some were just beginning, and some had done it for a few years. It was a tremendous relief to me to find out that many other children completed the day's work in even less time than we did. I wasn't neglecting some important part of kindergarten: the nature of one-on-one instruction simply decreased the amount of time needed. It became important to me to see what styles other mothers used to teach their children, to give me ideas about what I could change and adjust. If I was having a difficult day, it was nice to be able to call another homeschool mom and get her perspective. My homeschooling experience has been greatly enriched by knowing other women who teach their children at home.

More than likely, your daughter or daughter-in-law already knows a few people that homeschool, through kids' activities, or church, or neighborhood contacts. When she lets them know she is considering homeschooling, they will give her information on support groups in her area. If she does not know anyone that homeschools, she can search at the library for newsletters from homeschool groups, or she can contact *The Teaching Home*. This magazine has an extensive list of support groups in every state, and can give her the name of the group closest to her. In addition, anyone can contact Gregg Harris at Christian Life Workshops for a complete list of Christian home school associations in her area.

The second advantage of support groups is the contact for the children. It is fun for my kids to take field trips with groups of kids—and be able to bring their family along as well. A homeschool field trip with kids of all ages and assorted parents is a great experience. It gives my kids a sense of camaraderie with other homeschooled children.

Last year we had a "Homeschool Awareness Day" at the state capital, and homeschooling families from all over the state attended. My third grader was awestruck that there were so many kids around that were homeschooled. In addition, when we have group classes, she can build friendships with other kids that are homeschooled. It is very important to her to bond with other kids that are home during the day.

The final purpose of support groups is legislative awareness. Most support groups have a phone tree, which can be activated when items that will affect families and children are being considered in the legislature. These trees can be very effective in getting the word out on such issues so that Christians can be aware of what is happening at a state or national level that will effect them personally. The newsletter that most groups put out can also serve this function.

A support group can play a huge role in a homeschool, or a minor one. But either way, no homeschool family should be working in isolation; there are many ways for homeschoolers to get acquainted with other homeschoolers and help each other in their common task. Joining together with other families with the same goals can be one of the richest rewards of the homeschooling experience.

In summary, the process of beginning to homeschool may have many facets, but it is not difficult. It takes time and research, but it is interesting and exciting. Although the new homeschool mom will not become a homeschool expert overnight, before the first year is out she will be familiar with much of what I have presented in this chapter. At the least, her first year will be an informative and eye-opening experience as she dives into a whole new chapter of her life.

Chapter Seven

·····················

The Challenges of Homeschooling: From Diapers to Diploma

MANY WOMEN DO NOBLE THINGS, BUT YOU SURPASS THEM ALL. —PROVERBS 31:29

Perhaps by this point you have accepted the fact that homeschooling is indeed a valid educational alternative that can and does produce educated, well-rounded children that are at ease in many different kinds of social situations. You know homeschooling is legal and that there is no scarcity of educational materials. But perhaps you are still skeptical. Perhaps you have questions about your children's ability to handle the day-to-day challenges of homeschooling. "Can my daughter withstand the extra pressure?" you wonder. "Can the family afford it financially? How will they actually accomplish what they have set out to do?"

These are good questions. Homeschooling is a big undertaking, and it is wise for a family to consider the impact homeschooling will have on their lives, before they actually undertake the job. Let's take a look at some of these concerns.

Homeschooling and the One-Income Family

Home schooling is an inexpensive option compared to private schools, and many families choose it for that reason. On the other hand, although it is cheaper than sending a child to private school, it can be more expensive than sending him to public school. While families with kids in public school spend more on clothes, lunches, and sports than families that educate at home, homeschoolers must purchase their own curriculum materials. The cost of these materials, when added to the challenge of living on one income, can be daunting to the homeschool family, and you might think the combination of these two problems would prevent many families from choosing to homeschool. The financial demands on today's families don't allow many mothers to stay at home, much less manage the extra expense of curriculum materials. Nevertheless, families that homeschool have found ways to do both.

I know families that make great sacrifices in order to homeschool. The breadwinners of these families often make less than most of us would say is possible to live on. The mothers have skills that could be used at an outside job to bring in more money for the family, but they choose to use those skills within their families. These families do without such things as vacations, newer model cars, computers, nicer houses, and dining out. They live a simple life in order to provide the home life and education to which they feel God has called them.

I have heard some parents respond to the question: "How can you afford to live on one income? We would never make it!" with a sincere, "How can we afford not to? We are only given our children once, and we don't

118

want to put the job of raising them into anyone else's hands." Holding tight to this perspective will get families through the years of rough financial times.

Recently I was talking with a nine-year-old boy that has been homeschooled since kindergarten. He told me that his family had gotten snowed in while they were visiting a nearby city over the weekend and had had to spend the night there. He reported that they got a hotel, and that it was his first time ever to sleep in a hotel. Is he deprived because of this? No. He and his siblings enjoy a strong, stable, happy home life—without hotel stays, dining out, television, and other aspects of contemporary life the typical American takes for granted.

Families whose sacrifices are less than that of my young friend's family nevertheless give up a fair amount to homeschool, often doing without many of the modern fads and entertainments that make up the American lifestyle. I know many people will say, "Why? It isn't worth it. How can you deny your child a trip to Disneyland—or the video store?"

These questions do sometimes come into the minds of families committed to homeschooling, but the Scripture's view of sacrifice and the character they are building in their children keep them on the path they have set for themselves. Matthew 6:33 reminds us, "But seek first his kingdom and his righteousness, and all these things shall be yours as well." Mature Christians know that the time and effort put into their families is time spent storing up treasure in heaven, rather than on earth. These parents know there is no wiser investment than time spent on other people, and that there is no value at all in gaining more toys from this world. Most home-school moms know that they will not look back at their lives when they are older and regret the time they "wasted" on their children. Instead, they know that they will have given their children the most valuable gift of all, because they chose to devote their lives to teaching and training their children in righteousness.

Curriculum Costs

Curriculum expenses for each family will be different. The cost of curriculum can vary greatly, depending on the program and the publisher. Some families buy an entire curriculum and all the supportive materials, believing that doing so is a worthwhile expenditure of their money. After all, such families say, what is more important than a good education? Other families find it necessary to seek ways to cut corners and reduce the cost of books. For example, I frequently have my kids answer questions from a workbook on a separate piece of paper so that we can re-use the book. Using the library can cut costs considerably, and most homeschoolers are frequent library users. Used materials are also sold through homeschool support groups and newsletters. To save money, an experienced teacher can also learn to adapt material or simply create her own. As parents become familiar with curriculum and the way their children learn, they are able to design programs that are educational and affordable.

The Not-So-Hidden Costs: Personal Freedom

The personal sacrifices the homeschool mother must make are indeed great. As our society is not supportive of women that give up their own careers or personal desires for their families, often the first thing a homeschool mother must give up is caring about public opinion. I have one friend that shops at warehouses instead of grocery stores because, she says, she doesn't like to "stand in line and see all the women's magazines at the check-out stand." Wondering what those seemingly innocent magazines could do to such a strong, self-sufficient woman, I began to study the covers from a different perspective. I asked myself, "What do these magazines tell you about yourself? What values do they promote?"

I came to understand exactly why my friend went to such lengths to avoid them: those magazines promote a mindset that encourages women to satisfy their desires and pursue what they believe will make them happy. They tell women they are important, but not for biblical reasons: they tell you that if you are pretty, earn a decent living, keep a nice house, or are politically correct, you are worth something. According to these magazines, you should spend your time improving the beauty of your home, enhancing your physical appearance, and getting the most out of your sex life. Where do these magazines reaffirm the choice of stay-at-home moms? Where do they help women be better moms and wives from a biblical perspective? They don't.

Women who sacrifice their careers and personal interests to build a godly home are not praised in the media. They get very little support for what they have chosen to do, and that can be wearisome. Mothers who sacrifice comforts, and sometimes necessities, for the good of the family need all the encouragement they can get.

Fortunately, the Bible offers a lot of support for mothers who choose their families over their own pursuits. The following passage (and many others) demonstrates to stay-at-home mothers that all the sacrifices and efforts they make on behalf of their families are not only worthwhile to those families, but are important to God:

> Your beauty should not come from outward adorn-
> ment, such as braided hair and the wearing of gold jew-
> elry and fine clothes. Instead, it should be that of your
> inner self, the unfading beauty of a gentle and quiet spir-
> it, which is of great worth in God's sight. (1 Peter 3: 3-4)

Many women will need this reminder frequently.

Do You Have to Give Up Everything?

When I first began homeschooling, I came across an article
that discussed mothers and the changes they would have
to make in order to homeschool their children. In the section that discussed scheduling time for teaching the daily
lessons, the author included a list of various activities
women might need to give up in order to provide their children with the education they needed. The list included:

- Women's Bible studies
- Hobbies
- Church committees
- Shopping
- Taking classes
- Home decorating
- Political action activities
- Exercise classes
- Craft projects

When I read it, I cringed. I wanted to be a good
teacher for my daughter, but I didn't really want to give
up everything. (As it turned out, I didn't have to.) What
each mother gives up depends on her circumstances.

Some homeschool mothers need to continue their outside activities because they need the social interaction and mental stimulation. It wouldn't be a good idea for a normally very involved mother to quit every activity on her list in order to homeschool, because the radical change in her lifestyle would be difficult to adjust to, and because she might come to feel resentment about her new role as a homeschool mother. It would be better to whittle the list down to what she feels is most important and bow out of some of the extras, so she can still feel involved but not be so busy that she has no time at home.

Many people begin homeschooling their first child at the kindergarten level. Since kindergarten is relatively easy to teach—and only takes about two hours a day—Mom can ease into homeschooling without having to give up her activities. As the children get older, they need more time to finish their schoolwork (and Mom spends more time in preparation) but they need less supervision in other areas. At different points in the homeschooling process, the homeschool mother may need to evaluate her "extra" activities in relation to the needs of her students. Some activities may eventually be dropped for lack of time; others may be dropped because her priorities or interests have changed. After four years of homeschooling, I haven't given up a lot of the items on the list, but I *have* given up some of them.

Another factor that each homeschool mother must consider is her energy level. I once heard someone illustrate this idea so clearly that I never forgot it. She asked each woman to think of herself as having a little pool of water—the pool representing how much energy she has. Into the pool each woman was to put plastic eggs, one each for herself, her husband, and each of her children.

Some women find, when they have put in the eggs

representing their family members, that the pool is completely full—there is room for nothing more. Other women, after adding those "family member" eggs to their pools, find they still have plenty of room left, and can add outside commitments or hobbies without placing undue stress on themselves or their families. I have known women who struggle just to keep up with the housework and teach their children, and simply can't add any extra commitments. I have also known women who are able to maintain positions of responsibility that require a tremendous amount of time at church, in the community, or in a homeschool support group. God has made every woman different, and every woman must do what God has called her to do—no more and no less.

Organize, Organize, Organize!

A friend of mine stopped by several months ago to drop off an order for the food co-op. She rushed in the door, sat down at the table, and sighed.

"What a day!" she said, shaking her head. "I don't even have this order written up. I forgot I was watching a friend's children this morning, then I dropped two of mine off somewhere and didn't figure out how I was going to pick them up. I feel so flustered."

She scribbled down her order and wrote the check—for the wrong amount. As she got up and headed for the door, she exclaimed, "Oh! I forgot the baby was in the car! See what a wreck I am today?"

Once she realized the baby was still asleep, she paused on my front porch.

"I'm sorry you've had such a rough day," I said.

"Oh, it's my own fault. It's my disorganization that has messed me up."

My friend is a homeschool mother of seven, and knows what it is to be organized. Once a woman sees how important it is to be organized, she hates living without that smoothness in her day.

Many women cringe at the word "organization," but most will admit that they need more of it. The word tends to evoke the same response as the word "budget" —another necessity for the homeschool family. Both words sound rigid and difficult, but, in fact, both are tools that can mean the difference between a frustrating existence and a productive life.

A woman once told me, "I thought about home-schooling, but I realized I couldn't do it. I couldn't jump in the shower when I felt like it, or do what I wanted with that day. I would have to be much more scheduled, and I wouldn't like that." She was right: a homeschooling mom must develop a structure to her day that is conducive to teaching her children daily. Organization is important to every mother, but it is critical to a homeschool mom.

Contrary to popular opinion, organization is not a gift that some possess and others only long for. It is not something God gives to some people and withholds from others. Though it may come more easily to some, every-one can learn to be organized. Many of the homeschool moms I know admit that they have had to learn more organizational skills in order to effectively teach their children. The more organized a woman is, the more free she is to enjoy the teaching and the less likely she is to get bogged down in the details. Her family can look forward to school each day knowing it won't be a rat race of tying shoes, finding pencils, and searching for textbooks. It is simply easier to teach when the teacher is organized.

Where in the House Do You Have School?

Homeschooling doesn't require a lot of space, but there must be enough space for each child to work. Many families use the kitchen table. If this is the choice, then the materials must be well-organized: they will have to be put away at the end of each school day. Each child will have a box or basket that holds his books, writing utensils, paper, and other supplies, and each will be responsible for keeping his own box neat and ready for school. When school is about to begin, each child must have his box ready and well-stocked at his place at the table.

Some families prefer a designated school room, which can be achieved by allocating children and bedrooms so that a bedroom can be used for the school room, or by making a school room in a finished basement. Old school desks can easily be bought at garage sales or school district sales. The rooms can have all the trappings of regular school: maps, chalkboard, etc. A designated school room should be conducive to learning. It should only be used for school, and should be comfortable enough to work in. All the school supplies should be available in that room: having kids running around the house in search of a ruler is very disruptive to learning.

And the Housework, Too?

Since most homeschool moms teach all morning, they have half as much time to complete household tasks as they did before they started to homeschool. This can be quite an adjustment. When I began homeschooling, I had no idea how I would accomplish in half a day everything I was used to doing in a whole day. Though I still struggle over it, it *has* gotten easier.

A workable schedule is one that frees the mother to teach her children in the morning and do her household tasks in the afternoon, and allows time with husband and children in the evenings. After experimenting with different schedules for awhile, homeschool moms find one that works for them and their families. The schedules vary as greatly as the people who create them. What is important is that each family maintain a schedule that works for its members—a schedule that provides order and minimizes frustration and stress.

One of the most overlooked helps is the kids themselves. Children as young as five can be given chores that give Mom more time to do the things she needs to do. They can feed pets, clean rooms, or do simple housecleaning. As children get older, they can become responsible for the bulk of the housework. This is good training for the children, as well as a help to the parents. As kids reach their teen years, they can also share the meal preparation and planning. All of this frees up the mother to do tasks that only she can do.

It is important for those outside the immediate family to respect the schedule the homeschool family sets up. Mornings, or whenever your daughter schedules her homeschooling, are not good times to telephone. Though many homeschoolers do take phone calls during their school time, it breaks up the concentration of the kids and can be a distraction for the teacher. Just because a homeschool mom is home all day doesn't mean she is free all day. Because of the tighter schedule she must keep, visits and excursions need to be planned, rather than unannounced. Relatives who understand and respect the homeschooling family's schedule will be very much appreciated.

All-Day Discipline: Can It Be Done?

Many grandparents don't understand how their grandchildren will make the adjustment to relating to their parents as teacher. I am often asked, "How can they respect their mom as the teacher?" This question implies that the children don't currently have respect for their parents.

Respect is a critical component in the raising of children. It is necessary for children to learn proper respect for authority in many situations: at school, church, home, etc. Parents that cannot manage their children will have to learn to teach and gain that respect before they can begin formal teaching. In fact, there are homeschool families that have pulled their children out of public school and spent their first weeks establishing the authority of the parents in the home before launching directly into the books.

I don't think children's lack of respect is a good reason to avoid homeschooling altogether, though. If parents are afraid to teach their children at home because they are afraid of their children, they have some serious trouble ahead. The entire book of Proverbs—as well as many other passages throughout the Bible—makes it clear that undisciplined children are not the intention of God. God wants us to learn to honor him, and in order to do that, we must first honor our parents. If children learn love and respect at home, it will affect all the other areas of their life—as well as their future. Parents that are unwilling to teach respect at home will have a price to pay in the future that will be terribly high. Though some parents would prefer to leave that work to the schools, it is properly their own responsibility.

When the mother has the entire day to teach her children, she begins to see areas that have been neglected or overlooked in her children's behavior. Correction can be undertaken in many ways, but most will probably involve some negative consequences for undesirable behavior—some form of punishment—and rewards for exemplary behavior. I have used a wide variety of methods, from rewarding kind words with chocolate chips, to time-out, to a point system that discourages bad behavior, to spanking. The method used isn't as important as the fact that the children are accountable to the parents. They must learn to listen, obey, and treat others with kindness in the home. When my husband and I embark on changing a problem behavior with one of our children, we first identify the problem, talk it over with the child, and then develop a system of rewards and punishments that corresponds to that problem. When appropriate, we also use Bible passages that relate to that behavior. Then it is up to us, as parents, to remain consistent in the follow-up until we see improvement in that area.

Many books have been written on the subject of child discipline (see the appendix for some good titles). Most of the work of gaining control in the home will focus on helping children to understand that the parent is the authority, and that that authority must be respected. This can sometimes be accomplished by a good lecture on the first day of school, setting the tone for the year. More likely, however, there will be a period of testing. A child who has not had Mom as a teacher before will have to test the limits to see where the boundaries are. The first few weeks will be critical ones to such a family, as the children learn that disobeying their parents is not an option.

I have read articles about and spoken with former public school teachers that have left teaching and gone into other fields of work. Many of them say that they got out of the public schools because of problems with discipline. Although they enjoyed teaching, they got tired of focusing on problem behavior instead of on learning. This can be avoided in the home school, if consistent discipline is applied from the beginning.

That is not to say that discipline problems will not exist in homeschools. On the contrary, sometimes a whole lesson will be put aside when a negative behavior gets in the way of teaching. Many homeschooling moms have stories about having to put a lesson on hold and switching to a character training lesson.

My second-born child is a good case in point. Organization and neatness are not her strengths. One morning before school I noticed that her room was a disaster. I had two choices: I could ignore it and begin school on time, or I could tell her to go clean her room and we would start without her. I wasn't satisfied with either choice, because neither one seemed to correct the problem.

So I took them all to the school room and we reviewed some Bible verses on orderliness. From there we went upstairs and I worked on teaching her the proper way to straighten her room. I then gave each child the job of grading her room, A, B, or C. This wasn't in our lesson books, but it still taught an important lesson.

Other moms have conducted similar training sessions on such character traits as kindness or diligence. Although we will never attain perfection in these areas, homeschooling allows parents the time and flexibility to work on character training.

In fact, grandparents can play an important role in this process. You may not agree with every rule or behavior your children require of your grandchildren. (My mother says that the beauty of grandparenting is that she doesn't have to do much of the discipline.) However, you can enforce rules already made, and encourage obedience to the parents. You can tell stories about how you learned to obey when you were a child, and let the kids know how proud you are when they act in a responsible way. Kids raised in this environment develop much better respect for their elders. They see that rules are made to be obeyed, and are for their own good. When grandparents secretly encourage kids to question their parents' rules, or sneak them forbidden treats, they are doing nothing but creating confusion. The child is put in a position of choosing between people he loves, and it causes him stress. Grandparents who play a supportive role, rather than a divisive one, give a family a great gift.

Homeschooling for the Distance

"Mom, when will we get there?"
"In an hour and a half."
"Mom, how much longer now?"
"One hour."
"Mom . . . ?"
"No! We aren't even close. Stop asking!"

When we travel with our kids, they want to know how long they will have to sit in the car. For some reason, knowing how many more minutes are left seems to help the time go faster. If we have traveled for several weekends in a row, my kids stop asking how much longer it will be. Instead, they just entertain themselves and trust in the fact that we will, in fact, arrive at our destination. Then when we pull up, they say something like: "Wow! That didn't seem long at all!"

Homeschooling can be like that. The first year seems to go on forever, but after that the year can be over in almost no time. The length of time a family homeschools

131

is as individual as each family. Some families try it for a month or two, decide it's not for them, and return to public schools. Some families teach all of their children at home for all of their schooling years, and then do correspondence schools for college! The rest fall somewhere in between these two ends of the spectrum.

Most people that homeschool begin in the elementary years. Many more of these people are now graduating high schoolers from their home schools. According to the study *Marching To The Beat of Their Own Drum*, 65 percent of homeschooled students are between five and eleven years old.[1] As the homeschooling movement grows, that percentage will begin to include the teen years.

Most people who begin homeschooling believe in its value and its viability. Although there may be some that decide they made a poor choice for their family, the majority find it successful. Some feel that certain children could eventually benefit from public education, while some keep them home for all of their schooling. One family I know decided to put their oldest into public schools at age fourteen because he wanted to compete on the swim team, and they thought he could handle himself in public school. This family made it clear to their son and anyone else that if they saw any signs in him that weren't consistent with their values and beliefs, they would bring him back home.

Each family must weigh its commitment to homeschooling based on what is best for the children and the family. I have heard amazing stories of women who continued to homeschool through cancer, the loss of a spouse, and other tragedies. The commitment to home education and the circumstances of the family must be weighed by every family.

Homeschooling Children with Disabilities

There are several books available about the home education of special-needs children, and these offer a more in-depth discussion of the subject than I am able to do here. The premise of these books is that handicapped children can be taught at home quite successfully, with appropriate education on the part of the parents. Since handicaps can range from physical to mental to emotional, and from mild to severe, it is difficult to generalize about the best teaching methods for these children. But parents can definitely be successful in training their special-needs children.

As David and Laurie Lanier explain, in their chapter on homeschooling special needs children in *The Home School Manual*:

> The first step in working with your special needs child is to recognize that you are, in all likelihood, the single best resource. You should not expect anyone to care for the child the way you do, or to the extent that you do. You must learn as much as possible about your child's problem. Draw information from medical journals, experts, popular books, support groups and any other good resource.[2]

Parents of special-needs children are uniquely suited to choose the best education for their children and to have the dedication and love it takes to carry out their plan. It is important to remember that special-needs children have probably had a negative public school experience, so simply removing the pressure and negative social interactions of the public setting could be a great boost to the confidence of such a youngster.

Can You Teach without a Teaching Certificate?

Before I had children, I was a public school teacher. So

when people ask me if I am a teacher, I can easily say "yes." Although that puts an end to the questions and objections, I hesitate to say it, because it doesn't help other homeschoolers at all.

Holding a teacher's certificate really has nothing to do with my ability to homeschool. The only benefit I receive from it is the legal authority to test my children and other people's children. Research indicates that there is no positive correlation between a teacher's level of education and the student's progress. In fact, " . . .[t]he educational attainment of [the] parent is another factor that is of interest to policy makers and some researchers. In three separate studies, Dr. Havens, Dr. Rakestraw, and Dr. Ray found no relationship between parents' educational attainment and the academic achievement scores of their home-educated children in Texas, Alabama, and Oklahoma . . .[3]

Who Will Teach Calculus and Chemistry?

Parents teaching subjects they do not understand themselves sounds like a major problem, but, in reality, it is easy to solve.

How do most children learn their subjects? From a textbook, of course. Thus, a parent faced with a new subject can learn from a textbook also. This takes more effort than some other methods, but it can be done. In fact, some homeschool moms will tell you that one of the joys of teaching at home is learning material they missed the first time around.

But it is not necessary to learn algebra or trigonometry if a parent doesn't have a desire to do so. Many older students take correspondence courses in these subjects, or do their work under the guidance of umbrella schools, or tutors. An umbrella school is usually an accredited school that monitors home school students and provides testing and materials. Christian Liberty Academy is such a school. When you enroll in their program, they send placement tests for the children you enrolled, and choose the curriculum for each child according to his level. They provide tests, which are graded by the school, keep the records, and issue report cards. Christian Liberty Academy also awards a high school diploma when the student has completed the program. This kind of program can help a parent who has difficulty with certain subjects, as well as provide leadership and structure for the parents.

The advantage of correspondence courses is that they can be taken individually. A correspondence course is closely monitored by a teacher, to whom completed work is sent on a regular basis for grading and comments. This can be a way of learning a difficult subject that neither parent feels prepared to teach.

Other options are video courses and satellite schools. In a satellite school, a child watches a live lecture that is being televised from another part of the country, and thereby learns from an experienced teacher. Many subjects are often available. Video courses provide the same kind of "live lecture" experience, except that the lectures are taped, so the student can schedule his own viewing times. In many states, students can also go to the local high school for one or two classes, without enrolling in the school full time.

In talking with other moms who have homeschooled older students, I have learned of another option with regard to higher level material: allowing teens to plot their own course. For some subjects, this option could, in fact, be the best approach to take. A young person that can learn a subject from books and resources has learned how to learn, and is well on the road to self-education, the highest form of education. One mother says that she believes that the sign of a good teacher is one whose students are able to teach themselves. This same mom says that her oldest daughter has much more knowledge of history than she herself has, because her daughter has taken off with the subject. This is truly exciting for a homeschool parent to see in her pupils.

How Do We Know They Are Really Learning Anything?

To those of you who are trying to evaluate your grandchildren's progress, I must offer a word of caution: don't make hasty judgments. A relative may quiz a child and, if the child doesn't have the correct answers, assume the child is not functioning at the correct level. This is a totally inaccurate and unfair way of assessing progress. The average person does not have any idea what should be expected of children at various age levels, and should not attempt to casually "test" a child to see what he "knows." In addition, a child who is being grilled by a family member frequently gets tongue-tied and cannot come up with answers to even the simplest questions. I discourage any relative from using this technique.

On the other hand, there are a variety of methods available to evaluate children's progress. One is to administer standardized tests, as has been discussed in an earlier chapter. Has the child been tested? If he is operating well below grade level in many of his subjects, there may be reason for concern. If not, then the academic aspect of the child's education will not be a problem.

Some parents pull their children out of public school when they see that they are hopelessly behind. These families will not be able to assess their children's status for at least a year, as there is so much catch-up work to do. If you are concerned about a child in this situation, I would not look for instant results. Instead, I would give the family a year or two before deciding the child is not progressing.

Another reason for low test scores is that the child may have some learning difficulty. If this is the case, and the mother is aware of it, she can use alternative teaching methods, and different testing procedures. Some children need a different testing format in order to do well.

But what if a child is simply behind? Perhaps he is in second grade, and isn't reading, or is in fourth grade and can't spell a three-letter word. In the section on teaching styles, I explained the concept of delayed learning, as outlined in the Moores' book, *Better Late Than Early*. Kids whose parents follow this approach will not master skills on the same timetable that other children do. But in a few years, they are likely to master those same skills in a much shorter period of time than the child who learned them at an earlier age. Giving the family the benefit of the doubt, and waiting a year a two before being overly concerned about the child, is usually the best approach.

An interested grandparent can purchase books that summarize what a child should know at each grade level. The Core Knowledge Series (*What Your First Grader Needs to Know*, etc.) has a book for each of the first six grades; similar titles are listed in the appendix. Study the materials available. Is the child just a bit behind? If so, that is not enough reason to interfere yet. Perhaps the family needs more time to bring the child up to speed.

A book of this nature can be a welcome contribution to the library of a homeschool family, as long as it is given to help and not to pass judgment. You can also ask if you can help by tutoring the child in a problem area, or by purchasing materials the parents could use to help with this area. Make it clear that you want to help the child succeed and not make his problem a point of contention in the family.

Chapter Eight

· ·

How Can I Help?

THEREFORE ENCOURAGE ONE ANOTHER
AND BUILD EACH OTHER UP, JUST AS IN FACT
YOU ARE DOING. —I THESSALONIANS 4: 7

Once again, the Smith family has gathered for its annu-al Fourth of July picnic. This year you've baked your famous lemon pie, one of your husband's favorites. As the two of you drive up to the picnic ground at Green Acres Park, you smile in satisfaction as you see the games already underway: a few teens and their dads have taken over the volleyball court and the younger set is busy with a game of leapfrog. As your husband parks the car, you eagerly scan the familiar faces.

"Look, honey! Robert and Patricia even came with the new baby. I was afraid she would send Robert by him-self and stay home with Benjamin."

He smiles at you before opening his car door. "I guess that means you'll have to hold him for awhile to give Pat a break."

You flash him a grin and hop out of the car, leaving the unloading for later. As you approach Patricia and the baby, Janice runs up and grabs your legs.

"Whoa! Janice! You're going to topple me over. What a bear hug!" Reaching down to hug her, you take her hand and the two of you walk over to Pat, chatting with one another as you go.

"So, Janice, how are your seeds growing? Are the ones we put in the north window growing faster than the ones in the south?"

"No, Grandma! You silly. You knew the ones in the south would grow faster, because they get more sun."

"I did? Boy, its a good thing you're teaching me these things."

Coming up to Pat, you put your arm around her shoulder and give her a little squeeze. "Hi, sweetie. How are you feeling?"

"Oh, pretty tired. Would you like to hold Benjamin for a little bit?"

"There's nothing I would like more."

As she shifts the little bundle over to you, you let go of Janice's hand and cradle the baby against your chest. Remembering the child at your side, you ask,

"Pat, did Karen tell you that Janice has gotten an A on her spelling test for the last three weeks in a row?"

"No, she didn't. Good job, Janice!"

Janice smiles shyly as she stands on her tiptoes to look at the baby. A minute later, she skips off to play.

"Mom, I can't believe you're having so much fun with Janice's schooling. Last year you weren't too enthused about this homeschooling thing. I still think it is a little weird. I'm glad Jonathan is going to kindergarten this year so I can have more time with the baby."

"Oh, honey, it has been a delight to help out with Janice this year. You know I would love to do the same with Jonathan. Maybe if I helped out, you could keep him home, too."

"I just don't think I could do it. I know it has been good for Janice, but I don't know about us. How do I know he would be socialized, and all that stuff?"

"We should talk about this. You would be surprised . . . "

Much later, you and your husband are sitting on your blanket, having liberally partaken of the picnic fare.

Leaning over to him, you say wryly, "Do you remember last Fourth of July? The day the bombshell hit?"

"You mean when you found out Karen and Eric were planning to homeschool Janice?" he asks.

"Yes. I can't believe now how I acted, but considering what I didn't know about homeschooling, I guess my reaction wasn't all that unusual."

"No, it wasn't," responds your husband, "but I think now you'd be the first to question it if they considered putting her into school."

"You're so right. I absolutely love being part of their home school."

* * * * *

There are many, many ways grandparents, whether living close by or far away, can uphold their home-schooled grandchildren and support them and their parents in their schooling endeavors.

Attitude Makes All the Difference

Supporting a homeschooling family starts with attitude. As I have already discussed, the biggest support you can give your son or daughter is that of your approval. Most families I have talked to say that simply having their parents behind them and supportive is the biggest contribution they could ask for. All of us are dependent on the approval of our parents, no matter what our age. Though we can, and frequently do, choose a path that is not in agreement with our parents, we still desire their approval. Of course, that endorsement can't be manufactured. If you aren't supportive, don't make up nice things to say to your kids. But if you can even be neutral and tell them you trust their judgment, that will go a long way.

When I asked Dorothy Ferguson what she would say to grandparents who are unsure of their child's choice, she replied:

> Do not oppose them in any way, shape or form. Let them work at it for awhile. Watch and see how it works out. Pray about it, because you don't want to cause any problems for your kids. If it is the Lord's will then your mind will change. You don't want to regret bitter words that you say now. Let the Holy Spirit guide your thoughts and talks to your children. The public schools just aren't doing the job that we had when we were kids, and you will soon be happy that your kids have chosen this path.[1]

Dorothy sees many ways in which her grandchildren benefit from homeschooling, not the least of which is that they are very close and truly enjoy one other. She observes that siblings in homeschooling families tend to be much closer to one another than they are in other families, and she says that homeschooled children are generally nicer to be around. She is so happy that her grandkids are homeschooled that she has to watch herself lest she become overbearing with her enthusiasm.

Homeschooling parents do not want to alienate their parents. They prefer that their parents quietly tolerate the homeschooling, never even mention it, if necessary, rather than openly express their disapproval, or become alienated from the homeschooling family. I have talked with too many families that are hurt and disappointed because of the parents' negative reactions to homeschooling.

The most harmful example I have heard about concerned a family with three boys. The grandparents lived fairly close, so they had plenty of contact with the kids. When the wife decided to homeschool, her husband's parents were upset, and thought homeschooling would cause the kids to receive an inferior education. The manner in which they expressed their disapproval was destructive and resulted in much hurt on the part of one of the boys.

During the winter the grandparents went out of town for several weeks. One of the boys was in first grade, and he decided to write a letter to grandpa and grandma. He wrote it up in typical first-grade style, and mailed it. A week or so later, he received it back, with all the spelling and punctuation errors circled in red. Needless to say, family relations have been strained, and the child still doesn't like to write letters very much. Do these grandparents have any idea of the hurt they have caused, or what they are missing by not being positively involved in their grandchildren's education? Probably not.

Fortunately, this story is an unusual case. Though I know plenty of families who have experienced difficulty in this area, grandparents are usually not this destructive in the way they express their opinions. Many grandparents begin to adjust their opinions of homeschooling when they see the children are doing well.

Families are given to us by God to give us the security and guidance we need throughout life. When we break off the relationship with our extended family because we disagree with their decisions, everyone involved is hurt. In the long term, it is better to overlook decisions with which you disagree than to let a rift separate the family permanently. When children are involved, it is much less hurtful to give the homeschooling family the benefit of the doubt than to cause trouble and division.

The Curriculum Fair

Attending a curriculum fair is a wonderful way to show your support for your homeschooling family. Not only will you get a better idea of just how many people are involved in this movement, but you will be able to examine the many resources that are available to homeschoolers. Every state holds at least one curriculum fair a year—and many have several in different cities—usually in the spring and early summer, at churches, hotels, or convention centers. I believe a visit to a curriculum fair can dispel almost every qualm you might have, simply because you can actually see the quality of materials your grandchildren will be using, and discover for yourself how many people are teaching at home.

The number of people, amount of material, and variety of workshops can make a homeschool convention an overwhelming experience for a first-timer. Perhaps the simplest and least expensive approach is to purchase a pass to the exhibit hall only. Although the workshops will not be available to you if you take this course, you will be able to browse through the materials to your heart's content. But be prepared! For even a cursory view of the materials, most people spend two to three hours getting from one end of an exhibit hall to another. The choice and variety of curricula and other teaching tools, books, instruments, projects, and programs is mind-boggling.

Although you will find plenty of extra-curricular types of materials that are fun and beneficial—enough to fill up your gift list for several years!—don't make those the entire focus of your visit. Take some time to look at the depth and quality of the textbooks and teaching materials in the core subjects (reading, English, writing, mathematics, science and history). Browse through the history books of different publishers. Read a few pages to get a feel for content, tone, and readability. Pick up a math text, and see how colorful and well-ordered the lessons are. Study the tables of contents in several texts to get a feel for the scope of topics that will be covered in a year.

Many grandparents' minds are set at ease by such an examination of materials. In fact, seeing the wealth and variety of materials available to their grandchildren is often what gets them excited about homeschooling. The core materials look so intriguing that it is hard not to get the itch to delve into them. Add to that a few math manipulatives, a science kit, and a musical instrument, and they find themselves eager for a chance to teach!

Polly Gilpin describes her experience at a curriculum fair this way:

> The mob at the conference center was terrific! Do all these people homeschool? Yes, they do and they were having such a good time sharing their thoughts on the various curricula (that word again). The speakers were great. It was like attending a large Christian rally.
>
> The workshops were so enlightening. There were at least three things my sister and I reflected on later. It was apparent that we weren't parents of homeschool children. We were asked, gingerly, why we were there by some curious people. A typical response when they found out we were with out daughters was, "Oh, how wonderful! I wish my parents would come. They don't think we ought to homeschool." How sad to think these grandparents are missing out on something very special in their grandchildren's lives, because they are in reality fighting against

them. When the Brown Home Academy has "Grandparents Day" we come out 100 percent.

Another experience my sister and I shared occurred one evening when several of the Wyoming contingent met in our hotel room; the chatter by these mothers left us wondering what they were talking about. I decided right then that homeschooling was a gift from God endowed on these women who were following God's lead to teach their little ones.

And that is my response when one of my contemporaries asks me about my grandsons being home-taught. They always say, "But I could never have done that." I don't think I could have either, except if I were blessed by God to do so.[2]

Helping Financially: The Homeschooling Extras

As the grandparents of a homeschooler, there are many ways you can offer financial help to your children and their family. Since even buying basic curriculum materials is a tremendous hardship for families living on a shoestring, the extra games, manipulatives, and reading materials frequently get bypassed. Your holiday gifts can be those much-appreciated educational materials instead of the usual toys and clothes.

If you have an interest in purchasing educational items for your homeschooling family, a curriculum fair is a good place to do it. Since most parents choose their curriculum well before the beginning of the year and probably already have what they need in the core areas, I suggest that you concentrate on some of those "extras" that many homeschool families can't afford. Instead, consider the math games, colorful maps, musical instruments, foreign language tools, art supplies, and organizational tools that could make wonderful gifts. Many of these materials look and feel more like toys than learning games, and will be enthusiastically received by most kids. For example, one year, my husband's family bought us base ten blocks—wooden blocks made into cubes, strips, and plates to represent 1's, 10's, and 100's for teaching place value. The kids have used these in a variety of ways.

Don't overlook the many books available, either. The market for Christian children's books has grown tremendously, and the quality of stories now available is wonderful. Browse through the sets of fascinating biographies of Christian heroes. Most publishers now print series of books, which make nice gift sets and are read over and over again. I have given my mother a catalogue of a company that sells Christian books for kids, with items circled that the kids would enjoy. This makes it easy for her to buy something they will like, and it reduces my book expenses.

Purchasing books for your grandchildren accomplishes several things. The first is that they usually associate that book with you. One of my children mentions who gave her a particular book almost every time we read it. It also teaches your grandchildren that you value reading. In addition, it can be a neat way to grow closer together—whether the two of you read the book together or you read it first and talk with your grandchild about it later. You can create a strong bond with a child by sharing favorite characters and books.

I am just now beginning to see how fun this can be. My ten-year-old is reading books that I read when I was a child, or that I would love to read now. A few weeks ago she was reading *Christy*, which is one of my all-time favorites. After every chapter she would run downstairs and tell me what happened, and we would talk about the meaning of what she'd just read. It is a privilege to share these times with children.

Books also make great gifts because each child in the family can benefit without having to physically "share." A book my ten-year-old loves this year will be just as appealing to her sisters in the future. Recently my in-laws gave her illustrated editions of *Heidi* and *Black Beauty*. She loved reading them, and they will be enjoyed by each child when she is ready. I can't thank my in-laws enough for gifts like these. Although the phrase "give the gift that keeps on giving" is greatly overused, it truly applies to a good book.

My children even have the blessing of their great-grandparents contributing to their education: my grandfather bought them subscriptions to magazines such as *Ranger Rick* and *Zoobooks*. These magazines are costly, and are a resource that we are unable to include in our book budget for the year. The gifts of these magazines enrich the children's nature studies, provide lots of visual knowledge about animals, and remind them that their great-grandpa loves them.

Many games have educational aspects that can be used to good advantage because they offer children a learning opportunity that doesn't look like "school," or something that is "good for them." Scrabble teaches skills in spelling and vocabulary. Other games teach counting and money, or offer a challenge in logic and skill building. You have to hunt a bit for the games that have some redeeming value, but they are out there. These, too, are frequently items that parents can't afford to buy, but would like their children to have. Computer software can also be a great tool for a family, but it is costly. My father has bought our children The Oregon Trail, math games, and other educational software.

Other out-of-the-ordinary gifts that have been suggested include memberships to the local zoo, the recreation area, or other clubs. What about a year-round pass to the local swimming pool? Gift certificates are another good idea. A family can have a grand time spending a gift certificate at a bookstore or a teacher supply store. Gift certificates are also available for museums and other attractions that can just be too costly for homeschooling families.

We have been blessed with grandparents on all sides who honor and respect our way of raising our kids. Whenever they want to buy them gifts, they ask us first whether it is appropriate. When they want to buy a book, they check the title with me to see if I approve. They are always respectful of our values, and reflect that even in the gifts they buy. Such respect is perhaps one of the greatest contributions grandparents can make to a homeschooling family.

Homeschoolers who have their parents' financial help know how fortunate they are. Grandparents that provide some of their grandchildren's educational materials can have the satisfaction of knowing that they have enriched their grandchildren's education and eased a financial burden for their own children.

Love and Encouragement

In addition to gifts for the kids, there are many ways you can actively support your homeschooling family. Since the homeschool family and grandparents may live under the same roof, a few streets apart, a few miles from one another, or in two separate countries, there will be a great variety in the ways grandparents can be involved in their grandchildren's homeschool.

Although grandparents that live far away often feel

that they are missing out on their grandchildren's lives, much can be done to bridge the gap. My own children have two sets of grandparents that are one thousand miles away, yet they continue to be close and to consider the children a part of their lives. It can be done if both parties are willing to take the time to develop a long-distance relationship.

Only a Phone Call Away

All of my children have their birthdays within the space of a week: April 26, 28, 30, and May 3rd. This makes for a very busy week at our house, and it can be hard for the relatives to keep up with. My youngest, who is three, has the birthday that falls on May 3rd. By the time the last birthday of the week rolls around, much of our enthusiasm for birthday cake and presents has waned, but she has been waiting for seven long days. This year her birthday was on a Friday, and we went out for pizza. When we arrived home, she was in my arms when I pushed the button on the answering machine to hear our messages. This is what we heard:

> Happy Birthday to you,
> Happy Birthday to you,
> Happy Birthday, dear Alexis,
> Happy Birthday to you.

It brought tears to my eyes to watch her face light up when she heard Grandma and Grandpa's voice singing to her. They had already made three long-distance calls that week, but they took the time to call the littlest one, even though she would never have noticed if they hadn't.

The most obvious ways of keeping in touch are by the phone and letters. Many people claim that they "just aren't letter writers." If you "just aren't a letter writer," it might just be time to become one! The alternative may be that you are shut off from what could be a joyful experience for you—as well as for your children and grandchildren.

Recovering the Lost Art of Letter Writing

Receiving letters and pictures from the grandkids can be a great way to keep tabs on what they are doing in school and in their lives. Writing back is the best lesson on writing your grandchildren can have. Many people complain that often children don't see the purpose of learning to write, because so much of the writing in textbooks and elsewhere never gets read by anyone and doesn't have any real destination, but is just words on paper.

Writing letters teaches children that writing does have a purpose, and that it can be an effective form of communication. Long before children can write letters to the editor or enter writing contests, they can practice their skills on letters to relatives.

I found a wonderful idea in an article called "Grandparents See The Light", by Roberta Ritter Womack in *Homeschooling Today*. The grandparent starts a few lines of a story, such as "One day I was walking and I saw . . ." and mails it to her grandchild, who adds some more and mails it back. When the story is finished, it is kept in a notebook and another is started. The author reported that as they went on the stories got more and more complex.[3] What a great way to involve yourself in the education of the children, and encourage their creativity at the same time!

Via the Computer World

In the area of computers the children may be ahead of you, but that can be a great motivator for children. If both of you have a computer, you can send e-mail to them for less than the cost of a postage stamp. They can receive your communication in minutes and respond just as quickly. You almost feel as if you were living next door. With the ease and low cost of sending e-mail, we now hear from the kids' grandparents several times a week. These are usually little items that we wouldn't bother to call each other with, but they increase the connectedness my kids feel with their family. Writing back to their grandparents, they also learn how to use a mouse and a keyboard!

Even if your grandchildren have a computer and you don't, they can type letters to you or draw pictures. This is good practice for them and often much easier for you to read. In fact, if poor eyesight is a reason you cannot correspond with your grandchildren, computers can solve that problem too. My daughter writes letters to her great-grandpa, and then we enlarge the font size. This makes it much more readable to him, even though he cannot write back.

Audio-Letters

It seems that in this high-tech age the cassette player is on the way out. Nevertheless, it is still very useful for correspondence. In the case of younger children, the parents can just turn it on while they play and record their chatter, providing you with the feel of their language and spontaneous play. Older kids can sing songs and read stories on tapes and send them to you. This is also a good way for homeschooled kids to practice making speeches and reading textbooks out loud.

The correspondence need not be one-sided: you can send tapes back to your grandchildren. In the November/December 1995 issue of *The Teaching Home*, there was a special section on extended families. One mother wrote that she had asked her parents and in-laws to dictate spelling tapes for her children: the kids got a variety of teaching voices, and the tapes added enthusiasm to the spelling session. She reported that at the end of the list Grandpa would say something like "I hope you get an A!" and the kids loved it. Interest was increased in an otherwise dry subject.[4]

The same idea works well with regard to stories. Kids enjoy hearing stories read by their relatives. This can be done either on video or on cassette. My kids once lay on the living room floor all afternoon while we listened to an entire novel read out loud. I think this is a wonderful way of hearing a story, because the kids have to use their imagination to "see" the pictures.

A few years ago my husband's parents sent us a video tape they filmed in the fall. We live in Wyoming, where fall means all the leaves blow off the trees and the grass dries out. They live in Indiana, where the colors are glorious in the autumn. His parents took a walk through the woods and described the trees and sights as they went, filming with their video the whole way. The kids watched that tape dozens of times. They got to see trees that they have no knowledge of, observe hues and tinges that their imaginations couldn't fill in, and hear and see their grandparents. This activity would be especially meaningful if the time between visits is so great that children forget what Grandpa and Grandma look like.

All of these ideas for long-distance grandparents can be adapted by those who live closer as well. In fact, most of these ideas can be modified to fit almost any family situation. The next group of ideas can be used by any relatives, whether they live near or far.

Sharing Knowledge

Lisa Swigart, a columnist for *The Teaching Home*, recommends using the extended family as a teaching resource. She suggests listing the entire extended family by name, then listing each person's individual talents, abilities, employment, and place of residence. Each family member can then teach about his or her area of interest or expertise. This is a valuable experience for the homeschooler as well as the family member.[5]

Most grandparents have lived through historical events that the grandchildren don't know anything about. Putting your memories of the events of your life, both good and bad, will be a tremendous learning experience for your grandchildren. If you are a good storyteller, you can retell events in a dramatic way that will make history come alive for the kids. Or you can simply tell them what life was like when you were a child. Though we all joke about the phrase "When I was your age . . . ," it can truly be a great start to a teaching tape.

Scrapbooks and Other Projects

Many grandparents don't feel their grandchildren are doing much work if they don't see tangible results: graded papers and school projects. This thinking needs to be modified a bit, because much of public school work is needless busy work. Just because a child produces a paper does not mean he has learned something. In fact, it can be much easier for a child to fill in a worksheet with multiple choice questions than to explain in complete sentences the answers to the questions.

Although much of a homeschooler's work is done orally, there will still be plenty of papers and projects for the grandparents to see. Many families I know keep a scrapbook of photos and other memorabilia that they collect during the year. The pictures are used to tell a story about what the kids learned that year and where they went. My kids keep a three-ring notebook for the year, with tab dividers for each subject. Completed papers, tests, art pictures, and Bible verses all go into this book. This is a simple way for the grandparents to know what we are doing.

If you don't visit often enough to view the work, you can ask your family to copy certain pages, or take pictures of projects for you to look at. Most children are prolific in their production of art work, and can easily send some to you. Kids are so proud of their work, and don't spend much time worrying about whether or not Grandma will like it. Take advantage of their enthusiasm and ask for whatever you want to see. An involved grandparent has a full refrigerator door!

Cost-Free Contributions

Homeschooling families need a lot of pictures on a variety of subjects for special projects. One friend of mine has parents who are retired, and have very little money. They cannot buy materials or contribute in other ways because of financial limitations, but they still do supportive things for the family. Last year, my friend's mother went through many magazines and cut out pictures on everything she could find. She then put them into envelopes, by categories such as food, animals, people, and so on.

Categories can also be determined by the subjects studied. The pictures will be used in various ways throughout the year—as science classification papers or for art projects. They are especially helpful for smaller children, who want to draw more detailed pictures than their fingers can manage. If you looked at my second grader's science book, you could see that she was going to study food groups, plants, and animal habitats this year, and make the groupings accordingly. This is a wonderful help to a family and saves the mother lots of time.

Pictures can also be laminated at a copy store, or covered in clear contact paper. My in-laws once collected huge fall leaves, labeled them, and covered them in contact paper. This made a terrific science lesson. If you have calendars with pretty pictures, you can cover a picture with contact paper, and then cut it into a few pieces. This makes a neat puzzle for kids. Be careful how you cut out the pieces, though: it will be harder than you think to put it back together.

The Homeschool Teacher's Aide

Another way to help inexpensively is to ask the homeschooling parent for a scope and sequence of the subjects she is teaching. Read the list and keep it with you, keeping an eye out for items that would help teach that unit. For example, almost every first grader studies farm animals. If you are at a garage sale and see a set of plastic farm animals, you will know they could be used by your grandkids. Knowing what subjects are being taught during the year can enable you to make important contributions to the education of your grandchildren.

Although I would check with the parents first, old appliances can be educational, too. If you have a grandchild who is always wondering how things work, bringing in an old phone, for instance, so he can take it apart to see the parts could be a much-appreciated lesson. Many moms do not feel that they have the time to do "extra" things like this, and appreciate someone else doing it.

Field trips are another activity in which a grandparent's help can be a great blessing. Homeschool groups schedule field trips with regularity, and although they can be great learning experiences, they can be frustrating for a mother with younger children. I remember taking my six-month-old on a field trip and lugging her around on my hip for two hours trying to keep her happy. I didn't feel that I participated with my older kids at all, and my arm was very sore by the end of the tour. If a grandparent volunteered to take a child on a field trip, it would be a great experience for the child and the grandparent, and would give the mother some time with the little ones.

Sending notes of encouragement and cheer can help the kids as well as the parents. One grandparent makes certificates for the grandchildren when they complete courses of study or special projects. Since grandparents "brag" on their grandkids in other areas, there is no reason to withhold that praise for homeschooled kids. Let people know you are proud of your grandkids and their accomplishments, and then let the grandkids know, too.

Another way of expressing interest and support is to talk to your grandchildren the same way you would kids that are in public school. Many of the homeschool parents that filled out questionnaires for this book said that simply asking "So what are you learning in history these days?" goes a long way. Ask what subjects they like, or how they are doing in math. It is an easy way to let the kids know you are on their side and interested in what they are doing.

The ideas are almost endless when you have a helpful and supportive attitude. The goal is not to be super-grandparent and try to take over the children's education, but to contribute in any way that works for you and for the family.

Two Homeschool Grandparents: A Model

Dorothy Ferguson and Polly Gilpin have found some unique ways to support their grandchildren in home education. Dorothy is involved in the local support group, helping out generally in whatever way she can, and she occasionally writes articles for their newsletter. Her participation in homeschool support group activities is a real encouragement to many of the parents. Another job she has taken on is that of co-registrar (with sister Polly) for the upcoming homeschool convention in Wyoming.

One of her favorite experiences as a homeschool grandma was that of attending the Cultural Arts Fair for Wyoming homeschoolers. Here, homeschoolers gathered to display and perform their various talents. Dorothy says of the experience:

> I was amazed at how many people came up to Mary Lou and said, "I wish my folks would be as supportive as yours are." This would bring tears to me. Oh, you people don't know what you're missing out on if you're not supporting your children, because it is such a joy.[6]

Polly describes her role in homeschooling as mostly supportive rather than active, though many would see her as quite active. She says her job is to add enthusiasm to the kids' homeschool: "Let's get excited about this!" She goes on field trips with them, and takes them to homeschool sessions of roller skating and swimming. She also oversees homework from time to time when she is watching the kids.

Along with the registration duties she has accepted for the convention, she is also treasurer, thus she is responsible for keeping track of not only the registrations but the money for the convention—no small task.

If Polly were approached by a grandparent who was skeptical of homeschooling, she would respond positively. She says she would ask:

> What are your concerns? If they are about the real world, look at what other activities they are involved in. They are probably involved in AWANA, 4-H, and Sunday School. If the concerns are with the scholastic part of it, you can't get better instruction than one-on-one.[7]

She says she hears people say, "I could never have done that." And she responds with, "God didn't tell me to do it with my children, but most homeschoolers do so for religious reasons. If God told them to do it, he will give them the wherewithal to complete the task."[8]

Like Dorothy, Polly says the most important thing she can do is to be supportive. She thinks it is getting easier to support homeschoolers because the opposition is decreasing. But she also adds that she wishes she could help financially. She knows that the books and materials for homeschooling are expensive, and that if grandparents can help with those expenses, it would relieve some of the burden for the homeschooling family.

What About You?

Can you help with the homeschooling of your grandchildren? The answer is really up to you. By reading this book, and taking the time to understand the home-schooling option, you have done the most helpful thing a grandparent can do: you have become informed about and hopefully supportive of the job your children have taken up.

I believe that ultimately you will be very glad your children chose to homeschool their children. And you will be the fortunate grandparent if you choose to step in and take a participatory role in that school. Although your grandchildren will be better off for the experience of having Grandma or Grandpa take an active part of their lives, it will be you who receives the richest reward.

The Bible verse in the introduction to this book states: "Children's children are a crown to the aged, and parents are the pride of their children." (Proverbs 17:6) I hope and pray that your grandchildren are your crown, and that your children can look upon you with pride, knowing you are their fondest support.

Appendix
· · · · · · · · · · · · · · · ·

Resources for the Homeschool Teacher

There is no shortage of reference or curriculum material for those wishing to teach their children at home. Just a list of such resources would fill many pages. This appendix has been provided to offer you a starting point. Listed are several excellent books on homeschooling in general, well-known curriculum evaluation texts, books on parenting, major curriculum publishers and distributors, magazines for homeschoolers, and various homeschooling organizations.

Books on Homeschooling in General

The books in this section are some of my favorites. They are available at your local Christian or general trade bookstore or through homeschool supply catalogs.

Better Late Than Early, by Raymond and Dorothy Moore, The Moore Foundation.

The Christian Home School by Gregg Harris, Noble Publishing Associates.

Classical Education and the Home School, by Douglas Wilson, Wesley Callihan, and Douglas Jones, Canon Press.

The Core Curriculum Series: *What Your First Grader Needs To Know* by Ed Hirsch, Doubleday.

The series contains a book for each of the first six grades.

For the Children's Sake: Foundations of Education for Home and School by Susan Schaeffer Macaulay, Crossway Books.

A classic. Presents many of Charlotte Mason's principles of education. Highly recommended.

Government Nannies: The Cradle-To-Grave Agenda of Goals 2000 and Outcome Based Education by Cathy Duffy, Noble Publishing Associates.

A detailed explanation and analysis of the mandates and effects of the Goals 2000 legislation. Recommended.

Home Education: Rights and Reasons by John Whitehead and Alexis Irene Crow, Crossway Books.

Home Education With Confidence by Rick and Marilyn Boyer, The Learning Parent.

Home Style Teaching, by Raymond and Dorothy Moore, Word Books.

Homeschooling Children With Special Needs by Sharon C. Hensley, Noble Publishing Associates.

The How and Why of Home Schooling by Ray E. Ballmann, Crossway Books.

Good introduction to home schooling.

Is Public Education Necessary? by Samuel Blumenfeld, The Paradigm Co.

An excellent history of education in the United States, detail-

ing the rise of public schooling and spread of the humanistic philosophy of John Dewey and other influential educators.

Let the Authors Speak, by Carolyn Hatcher, Old Pinnacle Publishing.

An excellent resource for anyone working with living books and/or designing curriculum or developing unit studies.

Recovering the Lost Tools of Learning by Douglas Wilson, Crossway Books.

An excellent evaluation of and apologia for the classical approach to homeschooling.

The Relaxed Home School by Mary Hood, Ambleside Educational Press.

The Right Choice: The Incredible Failure of Public Education and the Rising Hope of Homeschooling, by Christopher Klicka. Noble Publishing Associates.

An excellent resource and reference for new homeschoolers. Recommended.

The Socialization Trap: Protecting Your Children from Age Segregation and Other Pitfalls by Rick Boyer, The Learning Parent.

A Survivor's Guide to Homeschooling, by Luanne Shackelford and Susan White, Crossway Books.

Anecdotal and humorous. Helps with the February doldrums.

Teaching Children: A Curriculum Guide to What Children Need to Know at Each Level Through Sixth Grade by Diane Lopez, Crossway Books.

An excellent curriculum guide, emphasizing the "Child Light" approach and drawn from the philosophy of Charlotte Mason.

Whole Hearted Child: Home Education Handbook by Clay
   and Sally Clarkson, Whole Heart Ministries.

You Can Teach Your Child Successfully (Grades 4-8) by
   Ruth Beechick, Arrow Press.

> *Full of down-to-earth advice and encouragement from an
> experienced educator and supporter of homeschooling.*

Curriculum Review Books

There are several excellent books dedicated entirely to
reviewing and evaluating homeschool material; their
authors, usually homeschool teachers themselves, have
spent a great deal of time carefully evaluating the myriad
resources available to people that school their children at
home. These books are excellent references for both the
novice and the experienced homeschool teacher.

Big Book of Home Learning (4 vols.) by Mary Pride,
   Crossway Books.

> *Many people consider Mary Pride THE expert on home-
> schooling material. Not only does she review thousands of
> homeschooling products, she also gives information on educa-
> tional computer software. An excellent gift for a new home-
> schooler.*

*Christian Home Educator's Curriculum Manual (2 vol.:
   Elementary and Junior/Senior High)* by Cathy Duffy,
   Home Run Enterprises.

> *A comprehensive curriculum manual, one volume for the ele-
> mentary grades, one for the secondary grades. It is complete,
> and pithy—a very good alternative to Mary Pride's more
> voluminous work.*

Books on Parenting/Child Development

And Then I Had Kids by Susan Alexander Yates, Wolgemuth & Hyatt.

Hints on Child Training by H. Clay Trumbull, Great Expectations Book Company.

How To Really Love Your Child by Ross Campbell, Victor Books.

The Strong-Willed Child by James Dobson, Tyndale House Publishers.

Major Curriculum Companies

A Beka Book® Publishers, Box 18000, Pensacola, FL 32523-9160

> *A Beka is one of the leading publishers of Christian textbooks, grades K-12, for use in the traditional approach. They have texts for every subject, all with a strong Christian perspective. Their material is challenging and fast-paced, with more than enough practice work and drill.*

Alpha Omega Publications, P. O. Box 3153, Tempe, AZ 85280-3153

> *Alpha Omega distributes a biblically-based curriculum. A full year's subject material is divided into ten "worktexts" called LIFEPACs, which are designed to be primarily self-teaching.*

Bob Jones University Press, Greenville, SC 29614

> *BJU has a complete line of textbooks, K-12, and supplementary materials. They have a different approach than A Beka® in some subjects, but basically cover the same scope and sequence. Our family enjoys Bob Jones University Press*

because the presentations of material are colorful and easy to follow, and there is very little busy work.

Modern Curriculum Press, Simon and Schuster, Inc., 250 James Street, Morristown, NJ 07960-1918

Rod and Staff Publishers, Inc., Crockett, KY 41413-0003

Rod and Staff offers curriculum in a variety of subjects from a Mennonite perspective. Though their books reflect that viewpoint, many non-Mennonite people use them in their teaching. They are not as flashy and colorful as many publishers—simple and basic is their approach. Their basic readers are unique: they consist of Bible stories, written at a progressively more advanced level.

Sonlight Curriculum, Ltd., 8121 South Grant Way, Littleton, CO 80122.

Their catalog describes the Sonlight curriculum as a "literature-based, unit study approach to history, motivated by a heart for the world."

Satellite, Umbrella, and Correspondence Schools

The Academy of Home Education, Greenville, SC 29614 (864) 242-5100 Ext. 2047

This program is aimed at junior and senior high students and provides the family with testing, record keeping, grade reporting, formal transcripts, a high school diploma, and more.

Calvert School, Dept. 2CCM, 105 Tuscany Road, Baltimore, MD 21210-9988 (410) 243-6030

One of the oldest correspondence schools, and long used by the children of diplomats, Calvert School has also attracted many domestic homeschoolers that have found Calvert's academically rigorous program suited to their needs. Testing available, but the materials for each grade are standard for all

*students in that grade. Testing/record-keeping and non-testing/
non record-keeping programs available.*

Christian Liberty Academy, 502 West Euclid Avenue, Arlington Heights, IL 60004

*When children enroll in this satellite school, Christian Liberty
Academy (CLASS) mails the family placement tests for each
child. Upon evaluation of the tests, they choose and mail curriculum appropriate to each child's level in the various subjects. They use material from a variety of sources, with one
charge for the whole set. Testing/record-keeping and non-test-
ing/non record-keeping programs available.*

Catalogues, Magazines, and Book Clubs

Conservative Book Club 33 Oakland Avenue, Harrison, NY 10528

*This club has recently begun to reach out to a specifically
homeschooling membership.*

God's World Publications, P. O. Box 2330, Ashville, NC 28802

*Offers a "Christian" weekly reader for various grade levels,
an excellent adult weekly news magazine, and a book club for
children that makes available high quality books that explore
many aspects of God's creation and human experience, as
well as other educational products.*

Great Christian Books, 229 South Bridge Street, Elkton, MD 21922-8000

*A good resource for curriculum, books, and materials. Most
items are sold at a discount, and there is a wide variety of
product. One of the nicest things about GCB is that they sell
so many Christian books and classics at discount prices that it
makes building a quality library possible, rather than something to just dream about.*

Homeschooling Book Club, 1000 East Huron, Milford, MI 48381 (810) 685-8773

Homeschooling Magazines

Home School Times, P. O. Box 2807, Napa, California 94558-0280

Homeschooling Today, P. O. Box 1425, Melrose, FL 32666

Practical Homeschooling and *Home Life,* Box 1250, Fenton, MO 63026-1850

> *This magazine complements* The Teaching Home *nicely, from a different perspective. It covers many different approaches to education, and contains lots of product reviews and "diaries" of other homeschoolers. Home Life also publishes* Homeschool PC, *a magazine just for homeschoolers who want to learn more about computers in their schooling.*

The Teaching Home, Box 20219, Portland, OR 97294

> *This magazine is a popular and well respected help to homeschoolers. It contains notes and ideas from other homeschoolers, updates on the legal situation (relating to homeschooling) in each state, and features an in-depth section on various topics pertaining to home education, e.g., teaching reading, etc.*

Homeschool Organizations

Home School Legal Defense Association, P. O. Box 159 Paeonian Springs, VA 22129

National Home Education Research Institute, Western Baptist College, 5000 Deer Park Drive SE, Salem, OR 97301

Selected Bibliography

Ambroll, Sueann Robinson, *Child Development*. 2d ed. New York: Holt, Rinehart, and Winston, 1978.

Boyer, Rick and Marilyn. *Home Educating with Confidence*. Elkton, MD: Homeschool Press, 1995.

Dobson, James. *Dr. Dobson Answers Your Questions*. Wheaton, IL: Tyndale House Publishers, 1982.

Duffy, Cathy. *Government Nannies: The Cradle-To-Grave Agenda of Goals 2000 and Outcome Based Education*. Gresham, OR: Noble Publishing Associates, 1995.

Klicka, Christopher. *The Right Choice: The Incredible Failure of Public Education and the Rising Hope of Home Schooling*. Gresham, OR: Noble Publishing Associates, 1992.

Moore, Raymond and Dorothy. *Better Late Than Early*. Camas, WA: The Moore Foundation, 1975.

Ray, Brian D. *Marching to the Beat of Their Own Drum; A Profile of Home Education Research*. Paeonian Springs, VA: Home School Legal Defense Association, 1992.

Wade, Theodore E. *The Home School Manual*. Niles, MI: Gazelle Publications, 1995.

Endnotes

....

CHAPTER ONE

1. "Positive Home-School Research Accumulates," *The Teaching Home* 14 (March/April 1996): 28.

2. "Test Scores of 16,320 Students Continue to Confirm Home-School Research," *The Teaching Home* 13 (March/April 1995): 27.

3. Brian D. Ray, *Marching to the Beat of Their Own Drum; A Profile of Home Education Research* (Paeonian Springs, VA: Home School Legal Defense Association, 1992), 10. (Similar findings available from National Home Education Research Institute, 5000 Deer Park Drive, S. E., Salem, OR. 97301.)

4. Michael Mandel et. al. "Will Schools Ever Get Better?" *Business Week*, 17 April 1995, 64.

5. Sarah Bryan Miller, "A Home Cure for School-Induced Funk," *Wall Street Journal*, 13 December 1995.

6. James Dobson, *Focus on the Family Newsletter*, December 1991, 3.

7. Christopher Klicka, *The Right Choice: The Incredible Failure of Public Education and the Rising Hope of Home Schooling* (Gresham, OR: Noble Publishing Associates, 1992), 46-47.

8. Ibid., 63.

9. Ibid.

10. Cathy Duffy, *Government Nannies: The Cradle-To-Grave Agenda of Goals 2000 and Outcome Based Education* (Gresham, OR: Noble Publishing Associates, 1995), 69.

11. Ibid., 71.

12. Ibid., 81.

13. Albert Shanker, "Where We Stand: Outrageous Outcomes," syndicated column, written under the auspices of the New York State United Teachers and the American Federation of Teachers, Washington, D.C., 1993, quoted in Cathy Duffy, *Government Nannies* (Gresham, OR: Noble Publishing Associates, 1992), 77.

14. Gregory Cizek, "On the Disappearance of Standards," *Education Week*, 10 November 1993, 32, quoted in Cathy Duffy, *Government Nannies* (Gresham, OR: Noble Publishing Associates, 1992), 77.

15. Duffy, *Nannies*, 87.

16. Dobson, *Newsletter*, May 1994, 1.

17. Cal Thomas in Dobson, *Newsletter*, May 1994, 1.

18. Duffy, *Nannies*, 7.

19. Ibid., 9.

20. Ibid., 14.

21. Ibid., 27.

22. Dobson, *Newsletter*, May 1994, 1-4.

23. Michael Farris, "More Than the Department—It's Time to Abolish the Federal Role in Education, *The Home School Court Report* 11 (Spring 1995): 3.

24. John Gatto, *Dumbing Us Down*, (Philadelphia: New Society Publishers, 1992), 26, quoted in Christopher Klicka, *The Right Choice: The Incredible Failure of Public Education and the Rising Hope of Home Schooling* (Gresham, OR: Noble Publishing Associates, 1992), 91.

CHAPTER TWO

1. Our Readers Write, *The Teaching Home* 13 (November/December 1995): 5.

2. Rick and Marilyn Boyer, *Home Education with Confidence* (Rustburg, VA: The Learning Parent), 21.

3. Jeff and Marge Barth, "The Blessings of Homeschooling" (audiocassette), n.p., n.d.

4. Our Readers Write, *The Teaching Home* 13 (March/April 1995): 57-59.

CHAPTER THREE

1. Klicka, *Right Choice*, 79.

2. Judy Hull Moore, *Our American Heritage* (Pensacola, FL: A Beka Book Publications, 1992), 146-147.

CHAPTER FOUR

1. Polly Gilpin, "A Note From Grandma," *CHALC Newsletter*, January 1995, 1.

2. Tony Silva, "Tongue in Chic," *Practical Homeschooling* 2 (Spring 1995): 96.

3. Peter and Cindy Heckroth, "Responsibilities of Christian Parents," *The Teaching Home* 13 (March/April 1995): 46.

4. Boyer, *Home Education*, 182.

5. Sueann Robinson Ambron, *Child Development*, 2d ed. (New York: Holt, Rinehart, and Winston, 1978), 323.

6. James Dobson, *Dr. Dobson Answers Your Questions* (Wheaton, IL: Tyndale House Publishers, 1982), 165.

7. Ibid, 172.

8. Lucy Maud Montgomery, *Anne of Green Gables* (Avenel, NJ: Random House Value Publishing, 1985), 87.

9. Theodore E. Wade, Jr. General Author and Editor, *The Homeschool Manual* (Niles, MI: Gazelle

Publications, 1995), 21.

10. Kathie Carwile Johnson, "Socialization Practices of Christian Home School Educators in the State of Virginia," *Home School Researcher* 7, no. 1 (1991), 15, quoted in Brian D. Ray, *Marching to the Beat of Their Own Drum: A Profile of Home Education Research* (Paeonian Springs, VA: Home School Legal Defense Association, 1992), 11.

11. Ray, *Marching,* 11-13.

12. Boyer, *Home Education,* 191.

13. Klicka, *Right Choice,* 134.

14. Boyer, *Home Education,* 195-197.

15. Ibid., 50.

CHAPTER FIVE

1. Klicka, *Right Choice,* 356.

2. Ibid., 239.

3. Michael Farris, "Legal News," *The Teaching Home* 12 (May/June 1994): 35.

CHAPTER SIX

1. Gilpin, "Note From Grandma," 1.

2. Moore, *Our American Heritage,* 93.

3. Brenda Kelly, "Common Teaching Approaches," *Christian Home Educators of Colorado Homeschool Update,* Spring 1995, 18.

4. Doug Wilson, quoted in "Columnists Face Off," *Practical Homeschooling* 2 (Fall 1994): 20.

5. Kelly, "Teaching Approaches," 19.

6. Jessica Hulcy, quoted in "Columnists Face Off," 20.

7. Kelly, "Teaching Approaches," 19.

8. Carole Adams, quoted in "Columnists Face Off," 24.

9. Karen Andreola, "Charlotte Mason Method," *Practical Homeschooling* 12 (July/August 1996): 33.

10. Joyce Swann, quoted in "Columnists Face Off," 21.

11. Kelly, "Teaching Approaches," 18.

12. Raymond and Dorothy Moore, *Better Late Than Early* (Camas, WA: The Moore Foundation, 1975), 34-35.

13. Kelly, "Teaching Approaches," 18.

CHAPTER SEVEN

1. Ray, *Marching*, 5.

2. David and Laurie Lanier, "Home Schooling Special Needs Children," *The Home School Manual* (Niles, MI: Gazelle Publications, 1995), 273.

3. Ray, *Marching*, 10.

CHAPTER EIGHT

1. Dorothy Ferguson, in an interview with the author, January 1996.

2. Gilpin, "Note From Grandma," 1.

3. Roberta Ritter Womack, "Grandparents See the Light," *Homeschooling Today* 4 (September/October 1995): 6.

4. Vonnie Green, "Relatives Read Spelling Tests," *The Teaching Home* 13 (November/December 1995), 46.

5. Lisa Swigart, "Extended Family as a Learning Resource," *The Teaching Home* 13 (November/December 1995) 42.

6. Ferguson, interview.

7. Polly Gilpin, in an interview with the author, January 1996.

8. Ibid.